FAITH
FINANCES

THOMAS E. ZORDANI

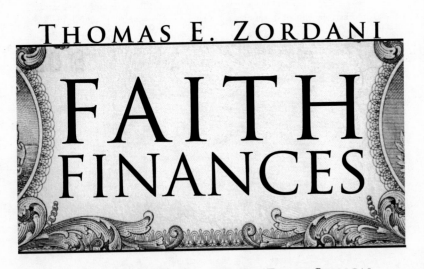

FAITH
FINANCES

A GUIDE TO MASTERING THE THREE BIBLICAL
PRINCIPLES OF FINANCIAL SUCCESS
IN EIGHT STEPS

TATE PUBLISHING & *Enterprises*

Published by Tate Publishing & Enterprises, LLC
127 E. Trade Center Terrace | Mustang, Oklahoma 73064 USA
1.888.361.9473 | www.tatepublishing.com

Tate Publishing is committed to excellence in the publishing industry. The company reflects the philosophy established by the founders, based on Psalm 68:11,
"The Lord gave the word and great was the company of those who published it."

Book design copyright © 2009 by Tate Publishing, LLC. All rights reserved.
Cover design by Kellie Southerland
Interior design by Stefanie Rooney
Author photo by Michelle Zordani of Zordani Photo

Published in the United States of America

ISBN: 978-1-60799-278-3
1. Business and Economics, Personal Finance, General, Religious
09.03.12

DISCLAIMER

All biblical references are taken from a single source—the Jerusalem Bible–Reader's Edition. I did this to remain completely consistent with scriptural translation. Some Bible translations are considered "very" loose when compared to the original texts (Greek and Hebrew). I disagree with an author who writes a book on personal finances that utilizes several different Bibles as his or her sources. The reason being, that I often see a listed passage that is used to fit the author's viewpoint and beliefs of what Scripture "should" say about the subject, not what it does say. I consider this to be a twisted form of biblical teaching. I do not want to imply or claim, in any way, that the Jerusalem Bible is the "ultimate" source of "truth" or "correct" translation, only the version I used for my research. This was also the Bible I had and used during *my* tribulations. This was the Bible I used to learn about finances.

I wish to dedicate this book (my first) to my lovely wife, Phyllis. She, often unknowingly, has fed my inspiration and drive. I am so very blessed to have her in my life.

ACKNOWLEDGMENTS

I wish to acknowledge the following people for all they have done in making *Faith Finances* a reality: First, I wish to thank my parents, James and Virginia Zordani, for the many hours they have spent helping me with the content, initial editing, structure, and refinement of my work; my wife, Phyllis, who is my biggest cheerleader and inspiration, without whose support this book would never have happened; our youngest children, Shania, Frances, and Jeremy, for their understanding of why Daddy could not spend as much time playing with them as I so desperately wanted, because I was writing the book.

I want to thank my brother David and his wife, Michelle, they contributed valuable and constructive feedback on the book's content. I wish to thank my oldest brother and best man at my wedding, Jim, for providing his inspiration, support, and guidance in my life for so many years. I would have never become the person I am without it. Over the past fifteen years, our older children, Angelique, Andres, Sabrina, Antonitte, and Rosalie, have experienced many of their own challenges, and I am thankful for their understanding and patience during the tough financial situation we endured in order to arrive at where we are today. I wish to thank my other brothers, Bob, Mike, and Kenny, who have provided much encouragement and support.

My faith has grown immensely over the years. I

believe this growth is directly responsible for much of my personal success. I have one very important person to thank for aiding in that growth. I wish to thank Fr. Greg Aimes, the former pastor of St. Peter's Church in Greeley, Colorado. His wise counsel during my darkest times helped me foster the strength I needed to grow my faith and meet and overcome many challenges encountered along the way.

I am grateful to my grandfather Donald Elliott, whose wisdom and insight helped shape my thinking on finances and helped me to better understand and appreciate one of the "greatest" generations of Americans (the generation that lived through the Great Depression and WWII). It is that generation that has set a very high bar defining sacrifice, discipline, and selfless giving. Our country needs to rediscover these rock-solid principles. Furthermore, I wish to thank my uncle Ron Stang, who was one of the first people to read my completed, but unedited, manuscript. He provided valuable feedback and support for my work.

Finally, I wish to thank my good friends Josi Brand, for her continual support through the years, and Katherine Burns, for her creative assistance in brainstorming for the title of my book.

CONTENTS

PREFACE

Why This Book?

I have chosen to write this book in the hope of changing the way people view personal finances, while bringing as many people and families to Christ (or back to Christ), as possible! Most Americans are occupied with a "just trying to survive financially" attitude. There is a better way!

Unfortunately, too many Americans do not possess the knowledge to lift themselves out of the mindset of financial survival to attain financial dignity, let alone financial security. Many have no idea how to access this knowledge, or worse, choose not to because they have lost hope! Regretfully, traditional education does not teach this information. It is difficult, or perhaps impossible, to teach your children something that you, yourself, do not understand. This book addresses this issue while using the Bible as its guide.

Our heavenly Father gave us a handbook for liv-

ing, known as the Bible. Contained in its many pages are wondrous and profound passages that, if applied, will provide blessings and abundance beyond belief. *There is no situation that the Bible cannot provide guidance about life.* One of the most discussed topics in the Bible is money. I have dedicated the last fifteen years to discovering and applying these passages to my life. The application of these passages entails eight steps.

The eight steps will correct what is most often the biggest mistake(s) people commit in handling finances. These are mistakes of priority. People often do not understand the correct processes that need to occur when working with money. The processes that need to change are spiritual, mental, emotional, and physical (lifestyle oriented).

> *"I had been blind and could suddenly see. I had been deaf and could now hear."*

Spiritual changes are needed because most people do not link money to their spiritual nature and well-being. Money is most often seen as being secular (non religious). If the spiritual connection can be made in finances, it will be more in alignment with God's purposes. This book addresses the spiritual changes that are needed.

Mental changes are important because the very essence of success in personal finance is mentally based. Attitudes and habits are the products of one's mental state. If this mental state is out of alignment, there is no possible way to be successful in your finances. This book addresses the changes that need to occur and why.

Emotional changes are important because finances are a very emotional issue. Jesus knew this. Consider the scripture of Matthew 6:19–21; it says:

> Do not store up treasures for yourselves on Earth, where moths and woodworms destroy them and thieves can break in and steal. But store up treasures for yourselves in heaven, where neither moth nor woodworms destroy them and thieves cannot break in and steal. *For where your treasure is, there will your heart be also.*

If the emotional connection is properly aligned, your heart will be in the correct place and your emotions will properly direct you on how to handle your money. Financial changes will occur because the spiritual, mental, and emotional changes have occurred or are occurring. The importance of these changes will be seen in the financial results. Knowledge and wisdom will be gained throughout this process.

There is a saying that states, "Wisdom is knowledge correctly applied." The reason these eight steps work so well isn't because I am so incredibly full of wisdom, because I'm not. I simply sought and asked for the wisdom contained in the Bible to aid me in my problem with finances. Consider James 1:5–8:

> If there is any one of you who needs wisdom, he must ask God, who gives to all freely and ungrudgingly; it will be given to him. But he must ask with faith, and no trace of doubt, because a person who has doubts is like the waves thrown up in the sea when the wind drives. That sort of person,

in two minds, wavering between going different ways, must not expect that the Lord will give him anything.

The reason the eight steps work so well is because they are God-inspired, and I simply found them.

Do not expect that you will become prosperous overnight, or that your money problems will go away quickly, because it is errant to believe that accomplishing anything worthwhile comes quickly. Christ's patience with his apostles transformed them. Such patience will change you too![1]

What can be expected is that by applying this process of change and committing yourself to growing as a steward, through study, faith, and action, will change not only your financial life but will touch *all* areas of your life. You must dedicate yourself to learning the stewardship principles discussed in this book, and set yourself on a path that is both demanding and difficult.

Part of this learning and direction may require that you endure many trials. The letter of James 1:2–4 says:

> My brothers, you will always have your trials but, when they come, try to treat them as a happy privilege; you understand that your faith is only put to the test to make you patient, but patience too is to have its practical results so that you will become fully developed, complete, with nothing missing.

When problems arise, get ready to rejoice,

because God is about to do something great in and through you! [2]

Becoming a "true steward" requires a great level of refinement that only trials can bring. The process of purifying gold is of this same process. To create "pure" gold requires several stages. The gold must first be extracted from the ground; often it is surrounded by various ores. It then must be separated from the vast amount of surrounding ore. The gold then is melted, using extreme heat. Because the ores and other impurities are less heavy than gold, they are slowly and methodically removed, until only the gold remains. This refining process occurs many times. Each time it is done, the gold becomes more pure.

The apostle James speaks of "spiritual purification" and refinement not unlike the process of purifying gold. Heat (challenges and trials) must be applied to remove all impurities. Neither gold, nor man, will achieve its or his true potential until this process has been completed.

You might be thinking, *Why are "these" eight steps so special?* There are numerous books available on the topics of finance, budgets, and investing. What makes this book special is, that no matter what your situation, no matter how little or how much you make, no matter what your age, these eight steps work!

I, as well as all of the other people I have counseled, are living witnesses that the eight steps work. All these steps are biblically based. Accompanying each step are numerous Bible passages that direct our actions, as to what we should be doing, or not doing, financially.

Many people who read or hear this information are often astonished. I have been told many times, "I have been a practicing Catholic my whole life. I have studied, or at least I thought I studied, everything in the Bible. I have to admit I do not recall hearing or reading anything like this before!" I felt much the same way at first. It was as if I had been blind and could suddenly see. I had been deaf and could now hear. What was it that happened?

My Personal Journey

My story began in late 1992. I had recently become engaged and would be inheriting a rather large step-family. I had some debt and thought it would be good idea to work some extra jobs, to earn enough money to pay off the debt and save some for the wedding. I began to work an unimaginable 155 hours a week. There are only 168 in a week. In addition to the 155 hours of work, I was spending three and a half hours each week driving between jobs, and another four and a half hours each week cooking, cleaning, and getting ready for work. I was sleeping five hours per week!

I cannot honestly tell you why I did what I did, because it had to have been the single dumbest thing I had ever done in my life, up to that point.

I was working without sleep for over four days straight. When I did sleep, I was never sleeping more than a couple hours at a time. I kept up this torrid pace for five months. After about three and a half

months I began to develop a strange rash. I did not think much of it at first, but after a couple of weeks, it continued to spread. It itched horribly. Nothing I did relieved the itching. It was as if my skin was on fire. I found myself not being able to sleep at all. The rash covered roughly 60–70 percent of my body at that point. I was later told that many areas of my skin were infected with staph and strep.

Early in the morning on February 25, 1993, I arose, walked into the bathroom, and vomited. I crawled onto the couch and remained there for the next two days. I could keep nothing down, and had a fever in excess of 105 degrees. I was incredibly sick. I did not want to go to the hospital because I had no insurance.

My fiancée was very concerned because my condition continued to worsen. After speaking to people at the hospital, she forced me to admit myself to the hospital. Neither of us realized, at the time, how serious my situation was. I was suffering from massive infections. I would remain in the hospital for two weeks before the infections were controlled.

I had immense stomach pain and was continually nauseous and vomiting. Nothing that the hospital provided relieved the pain and nausea. I suspected something else was wrong.

I had been in the hospital for almost two weeks and had eaten nothing; I was often in great pain. I felt the doctors were not doing a good job of diagnosing what was wrong with me. I began to tell the doctors that I felt somewhat better, but in the back of my mind, I was telling myself that I had to get out of the hospital because I was racking up thousands of dollars of medical bills, which I could not afford. What was the point of being in the hospital if they were not helping me? A couple of days later I was released.

I stayed at my fiancée's home for the next couple of days, never getting out of bed. I convinced her that I needed to head to Denver and my apartment to rest. She contacted my parents and made plans that I would stay with them instead, so they could watch over me.

I arrived at my parents' home, crawled into bed, and could not get up. I began to vomit small quantities of blood and broke with another fever of 105 degrees. My parents immediately called the doctor, who asked that I be rushed to the hospital. I would remain in the hospital for another two weeks. It was at that time a perforated ulcer was diagnosed, and once again I was suffering from massive infections.

I had been in hospitals for almost a month. They properly treated the ulcer and the infections. It was because of the treatment that I felt I was able to eat again. I had lost over forty pounds during this time. Before this incident, I had weighed 170 pounds.

The amount of medical debt was over $70,000. I had earned approximately $8,000 working all of the jobs over the previous months. I felt angry. I had expended all of that effort to pay off my bills, and now found the debt had increased over 800 percent.

I failed to see the fairness of it all. But this proved to be merely the start of my problems.

We proceeded with the wedding in November of 1993. I continued juggling the debts we had for the next year. Pressure was building financially. My relationship with my new wife was very strained. We were having serious marital problems, and I was in counseling with my parish priest. For failure to pay the rent, we were evicted from our rental home in Milliken, Colorado, in June of 1995.

With our marriage on the verge of collapse, my family and I homeless and in an unimaginable swamp of debt, I engaged in numerous counseling sessions with our parish priest about our situation. We talked about our need to move to Denver so that I could earn more money with my business. I thought my wife could find a good job as well. My wife adamantly opposed moving to Denver under any circumstances. We had been quarreling over this for more than a year.

In my mind, it was strictly an economic decision and no other. I owned an antique chair-repair service and retail business in Denver. I was spending three hours per day, in good weather, commuting from Milliken to Denver and back. My ability to produce was tied to the amount of time I spent working at my shop. If I could apply the three extra hours per day working, plus the cost of gas, and the wear and tear on the van, our finances would improve. My perspective was that if we failed financially, it would not matter where we lived, because in either case we would be homeless.

In my wife's mind, it was about her level of comfort with her life, about losing her identity, being near her family and her work, and the fear of losing her children to the vagaries, temptation, and trappings of a big city. She had been raised in the small farming community of LaSalle, Colorado (near Greeley); Milliken was a mere fifteen minutes away. She could not see the financial benefits of moving to Denver would provide. I, on the other hand, could think of no other way to fix our financial situation.

In what proved to be the last counseling session alone with my priest, he asked if I was committed to our marriage. He asked if I felt my wife was committed to our marriage. These questions greatly disturbed me. I remained silent for a number of minutes while I seriously considered my answers. The answer to the first question was easy. Yes, I was committed! The answer to the second was much more difficult. I hoped she was, but how could I know for sure? She had been married before. He asked if I had developed a plan to show her how everything would work. I had already done this.

He then said, "Well, if you are committed to your marriage, if you think she is committed to the marriage, and you have showed her your plan, then you must test the marriage." I would be placed in the very tough position of telling my wife that I must leave if she would not support the move to Denver. The priest and I discussed this position for some

time. I was terrified with what might occur. His only comforting comment in parting was, "Have faith!"

I thought about the impending conversation with my wife and how it would play out. I thought through every response and nuance I could imagine. I had a knot the size of a basketball in my stomach. I met her at her friend's house. We had been staying there during the night, while we were homeless. We had to split up the children to stay wherever we could find a place for them. Some of the children stayed with neighbors and some stayed with friends.

The actual conversation did not last very long. It went as I had feared it might. I was unsuccessful at convincing my wife. With tears in my eyes, I placed my wedding ring in her hand and told her I was going to Denver to find us a place to live and that I hoped she would follow.

I separated from my wife for about a month because she would not support the move to Denver. It proved to be very difficult finding a home when I had no money and horrible credit. Who would rent to someone who had been evicted only two months earlier? How could I afford a house in Denver when we could not afford a small house in Milliken for $395 per month? Most places in the Denver metro area, that fit our needs, were going for $900 to $1,300 per month, with a deposit equal to a month's rent and the first month's rent in advance. I had no money!

Many people ask why my parents did not help us. My parents simply did not know what was happening. I kept this hidden from them. It was not until I

called them to tell them I needed a place to live that they began to understand our true situation. This was a very humbling experience. Here I was, a married man, forced into asking my parents if I could move back home until I could find a place to live. After three weeks of no communication whatsoever with my wife, she finally called me, and agreed to join me in Denver, and to assist in finding a place that my parents would help us rent. I had to borrow money from them to afford the deposit and first month's rent.

Whenever I had free time, I read. I focused on the Bible. I read everything I could find on finances, books on relationships, faith, and self-improvement.

The Awakening!

After my hospital episode but before we became homeless I had been having grave financial difficulties. I had been feeling that I was at the end of my financial rope; there was an enormous amount of medical debt, I was having tax problems, and I had a number of pending lawsuits due to debts from bouncing checks left and right.

Quite simply, things were well beyond a mess. One day it happened that I was thumbing through greeting cards at a local grocery store. I picked up a card and a particular Bible passage from the book of Jeremiah jumped out at me. My eyes suddenly blurred as I began to weep. I looked around to see if anyone was watching. I could not control the tears. This passage literally reached into my heart and changed my whole thought process toward my approach to dealing with the Bible. It was Jeremiah 33:3. It read, "Call to me, and I will answer you; I will tell you great mysteries of which you know nothing."

It was as if I had just received a personal phone call from God. He knew exactly what was needed. This simple epiphany transformed my thought process. I realized exactly what I should have been doing all along. I needed to rely on him. I needed to seek him in my financial life. The only way to develop such a relationship is through prayer and the study of Scripture.

Through prayer and study, I changed my life forever. How could nineteen simple words have such a profound impact? Simply by asking, "Lord! Please, help me understand what it is that I am doing wrong financially! Show me what I need to be doing. Help me understand your way!"

The key to my success was calling out to God and believing his promise. Through the Bible, he would teach me great things I did not know. I sought knowledge, wisdom, and understanding (three of the seven gifts of the Holy Spirit). It was at that time that I realized that God knew my mind was open and my heart softened and that both were ready for his direction and purification. I began to pray and read the Bible every day.

I soon found yet another powerful passage, which spoke to effectively changing my financial situation through prayer. The passage from Matthew is probably one of the most recognizable passages in the New Testament. I was quite familiar with it from church, but I had never reflected on it from the perspective of finances. Matthew 7:7–9 read, "Ask and it will be given to you; search, and you will find; knock, and the door

will be opened to you. For the one who asks always receives; the one who searches always finds; the one knocks will always have the door opened to him ... "

I had discovered two of the most powerful passages in the Bible referencing promises made by God to fulfill our needs and then applied them to my finances. I knew that if my heart and mind were in alignment with God, my financial future would change. But I still had a lot to learn.

Do you ever remember receiving a love letter from someone with whom you were head-over-heels in love? The feeling you had when it came in the mail or was hand-delivered to you by an acquaintance, either yours or theirs? How, with impatient anxiety, you thought of nothing more than ripping it open in anticipation of what it would say? As you read it, your heart would race, reading and re-reading each sentence. The lines of written love hung in your mind and melted your heart; it was if that person were right next to you, looking into your eyes as he/she spoke his/her intimate thoughts. Nothing else mattered at that point. Is that how you feel when you read the Word of God? Does it reach into your heart and capture you? Do you hang on its every word? Christ wants for each of us to feel that way toward the Father.

People often ask me about the origin of the eight steps. The eight steps were inspired by the Bible, but really they are a product of what I would consider the worst time of my life.

Our Dream Home

In case you were wondering how things have turned out, I must admit that I am humbled by how God has seen fit to bless me and my family. We live in our dream home in a very nice neighborhood. Reminiscing about the journey to obtain our dream home often moves me to tears. I think of the fact (as of the writing of this book) that only thirteen years ago we were over $100,000 in debt and homeless. I marvel at the fact that God provided me the strength, the courage, and the faith so that I could envision what the future would hold for me and my family if I would believe in him and trust in him. Once I allowed him to occupy the driver's seat of my life, the journey proved to be amazing!

Let me share with you how I came to find our wonderful home. On Saturday mornings, I would often arrive at my shop early and walk next door to the 7-Eleven store to buy a newspaper, a doughnut, and a fountain drink. I would open the paper and

look in the real estate section to view the new homes. I would read about all of the wonderful upgrades and amenities and dream of when my time would come to buy a home.

I remember the first time seeing a picture in the newspaper of the home we would come to own. After seeing the picture, I decided to cut it out, and after my shop closed, I drove to the subdivision where it was being built. The model home was a two-story with a very large basement and a three-car garage. There were art niches that had custom lighting in a number of areas throughout the home. The front room, the living room, and the dining room all had vaulted ceilings and were wide open. There were three bedrooms upstairs and a spacious master suite! There were his-and-hers walk-in closets and a large semi-circle sitting area with three sides of windows to look out into the backyard. The kitchen had an enormous amount of cabinet and counter space with a large island in the middle and a wonderful breakfast nook for the family. I could not believe how spacious the house was. I just had to show this to my wife!

However, I knew that we could not buy the home until our debt was cleared up and we had saved enough money to afford it. The biggest problem I faced was that even if all of the debt was paid and we had saved 20 percent for the down payment, we could not afford the home with our then-current incomes. We would need to earn a lot more money to afford this house. Nevertheless, I continued to dream and plan for this. We began tithing during this time.

I would often go to the development and tour the model home and talk to the sales people to learn everything I could about it. They must have thought I was deranged, always talking about the house and asking questions about it. The most frustrating part about my visits was that every couple of months or so, the price increased. This process continued for three years. The price of the home had increased nearly $60,000 during that time.

During this three-year period, I sold my business for a modest sum and changed careers and went to work for a Fortune 200 company (I explain this story in more depth in a later chapter). My wife was able to secure a good job as a cosmetologist at an upscale day-spa. My income continued to increase significantly. Finally in January of 2000, we would become debt free and had saved sufficient money for a down payment on our dream home. We purchased our new home in July of 2000. We decided on very few building upgrades with the intention that I would make the wanted changes later.

Over a period of two years, with the help of my dad, we finished the basement. We constructed two additional large bedrooms, an in-home theater room, and a full bathroom, a craft room for my wife, a pantry, and several storage areas. We modeled the basement to look like the architecture throughout the rest of the home.

Our house sits in the back of a cul-de-sac. Our property is the largest in the subdivision and occupies almost a half-acre. We built a large bi-level

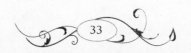

Brazilian hardwood deck, and a large built-in brick barbeque. The deck has an upper seating level in the shape of a hexagon (six-sided) that sits up to twenty-eight people around a four foot outdoor natural gas fire place overlooking a large sixteen-by-twenty-four-by-seven water feature. The water feature has a double waterfall that pumps twelve thousand gallons of water an hour into a twelve-by-fifteen Koi pond. I designed the falls to acoustically project the sound of the falling water directly into the second-story master bedroom windows. At night my wife loves to open the bedroom window and shade to hear and see the lighted falls. It is amazingly peaceful and soothing.

A third of our yard is dedicated to gardening. We have a number of raised planting beds for herbs, vegetables, berries, and flowers along with a small orchard of peach, apple, plum, cherry, and pear trees. We also cultivate grapes.

Back in the days of my antique restoration business, I frequently delivered chairs to clients in Aspen and many other mountain communities. In driving to these communities, I encountered gorgeous scenery. These trips were what inspired me to build the water feature I now have. I would take several photos of the rivers and falls every time I made the trip. Taking the photos would lock into my mind exactly what everything looked like.

We have not yet completed all of the home projects that we dreamed of all those years ago, but we are well on our way to having our home exactly like

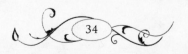

we envisioned before we bought it. I have no doubt, with God's blessing, *all* of our dreams and visions will come to be.

Everyone has a different idea of what is success and happiness. Everyone has different goals, dreams, and desires. The important thing is that you pursue them with passion. Don't pursue them for the sake of pride. Pursue them to glorify God and advance his kingdom. Remaining pure of heart in the pursuit of happiness is key to obtaining your dreams and goals.

It is my hope to inspire you to accomplish whatever goals and dreams you may possess in your heart. You are fully capable of attaining whatever your dreams and goals may be. Honor God by becoming the best person you are capable of becoming and utilizing your God-given talents to the fullest extent you are capable.

INTRODUCTION

"This, however you must know: I find that
God made man simple; man's complex
problems are of his own devising."

How true is this statement for your life? This passage was taken from Ecclesiastes 7:29–30. It is one of several hundred pertaining to personal finances contained in the Bible. Are the complexities, anxieties, and problems of your financial life summed up with that passage?

Are you ready for change?

When was the last time that you had something in your hands that worked 100 percent of the time it was tried—something that never failed? The information contained in this book will, if followed, change your financial life forever. You may be asking yourself how that is possible. Well, it is true!

This is not to say that this is the only way to change your current and future financial situation,

but it simply is the best, I have found. The many people I have counseled that strive to master these principles by following the eight steps, see unbelievable change and dramatic improvement in their financial situations. Everyone is different; everyone's situation is different, but the common thread with everyone who has practiced these steps faithfully, has been success.

The information contained in the following pages will impact your life for the better. People from all social/economic strata desperately need this information and will benefit from it. If it is followed!

Are you struggling or perhaps living a total and complete financial nightmare? Smile, and regain your hope, because this book is definitely for you!

Maybe you are retired or soon to be retired, on a fixed income, and feel there is nothing that can be done to improve your situation. This book is for you! I assure you, things can be improved!

Perhaps you have done a fine job with your finances or maybe not as good as you would like. Do you have family members, children, parents, grandparents, aunts, uncles, or cousins who are financially lost? Then this book is for you and for them!

Perhaps you feel that your finances are in tip-top shape; you make a lot of money and you have many nice things. You pay your bills on time and are able to manage debt and give in what you think is a responsible manner. Do you give the way you can or should? Perhaps you would just like to better understand what God expects of you as a steward.

If you died tomorrow and, as part of your acceptance process into heaven, you were required to have a face-to-face with God and if he required you to give an accounting of all that you did or failed to do, how would you fare? Romans 14:11-12 says,

> "We shall have to stand before the judgment seat of God; as scripture says: By my life—it is the Lord who speaks—every knee shall bend before me, and every tongue shall praise God. It is to God, therefore, that each of us must give an account of himself."

Remember, your answer(s) will decide whether you will remain with God in heaven or go to "the other place." Would you be confident that you had done *everything* God expects of you with all that you were given? Did you give freely from all of your resources? If your answer is anything but an absolute *yes,* then you need to roll up your sleeves and go to work. If you are unsure of what is expected of you, then read on.

A passage from Luke speaks to this:

> The servant who knows what his master wants, but has not even started to carry out those wishes, will receive very many strokes of the lash. The one who did not know, but deserves to be beaten for what he has done, will receive fewer strokes. When a man has had a great deal given him, a great deal will be demanded of him; when a man has had a great deal given him on trust, even more will be expected of him.
>
> Luke 12:47–48

This passage clearly delivers the message that if you are well off, it is required of you to know and act on what is expected of you. If you do not yet know what is expected of you, then this book is for you!

The truth is, I could compose a whole chapter writing about people's circumstances, needs, and how this book will help them. The fact is, no matter what your situation—single, married, divorced, widowed, engaged, wealthy, poor, or anywhere in between— you will find this book to be of immense help!

The key is that you must *act!* You must act with prayer, study, and commit yourself to change. Remember, God made things simple—we make things complex and riddled with problems. Those problems have solutions.

If you are interested and committed to changing your life's financial direction, either subtly, or radically, the path to do so is the same for everyone.

You must commit to mastering the three financial stewardship principles contained in the Bible. These principles form the foundation of everything a person needs to do to be truly successful in finances and become a "true steward." These three principles are:

1. Giving

2. Managing

3. Increase

The foundation of these three principles is the eight steps. Due to the fact that these three principles are so important, I do not feel I would be doing them justice, by attempting to incorporate them into the eight steps. I have chosen not to make this book about the three principles because you must first master the basics of those. The three principles will be a book for a future time. However, these principles are referenced frequently throughout this book. This book is about the eight steps and will set the foundation needed to master the three principles. You will learn and/or strengthen *all* of the needed basics for this foundation.

My hope for each and every one who reads this book and puts into practice the eight steps is that you gain faith and courage to face your fears, your doubts and your financial challenges, whatever they may be, head-on.

Families Are Losing the Battle

How is it that we live in the wealthiest nation on earth and 96 percent of Americans are broke; literally two or three paychecks from being on the street (my opinion)? A sad fact is that many people's definition of prosperity is the time from Friday's paycheck to Saturday's celebrations and shopping. [3] America has the highest standard of living in human history. Yet our beloved country's citizens are horrendously in debt. Savings rates among Americans have fallen into the negative category for only the second time in our country's history. The Commerce Department recently released a report stating, that the savings rate in all of 2006 was a negative -1%. In 2005 the savings rate was -.4%. The only other time this occurred, was during the Great Depression. Look around. Does this seem like the Great Depression to you?

What does it mean to have negative savings rates? It means that not only are American families

42

spending 100 percent of everything they make, but they are dipping into reserves and more. According to the most recent Federal Reserve study; it showed that 43 percent of U.S. families spent more than they earned. On average, Americans spend $1.22 for each dollar they earn (according to the same study). Many people are continuing to spend borrowed money for frivolous purchases. Many Americans are fully leveraged, or worse, in their home mortgages. They have little or no equity, or worse yet, are upside down in their mortgage. They owe more than the house is worth. Foreclosures are at an all-time high. Bankruptcies are at an all-time high. The average American has 7.6 credit cards, with most carrying balances month to month. The average household has more than $8,000 in credit card debt up from $3,000 in 1990.[4] It's costing Americans twice as much to live beyond their means as it did twenty years ago! [5]

Families are falling further behind financially. They are ill-equipped to deal with the economic challenges they are facing. They are not properly preparing for the future, and as a result, they are being torn apart by financial stresses.

In the 1940s and 1950s, the first widespread use of credit cards appeared. [6] The issuance of credit cards enticed families to begin making frequent purchases on credit, rather then paying with cash. Since the 1950s, the American family has begun a major shift from a one-parent (usually the father) working family, to a two-parent working family. Today, it is too often a necessity that both parents work, to stay afloat

financially. American families could probably live on next to nothing, if only the neighbors lived on less. [7] Is this damaging situation a mere coincidence? No!

The two major contributors to both parents needing to work phenomenon are taxation and the issuance of credit. If necessity forces both parents to work, who then is raising the children? This problem has given the government the ability to diminish the role of parents raising their children. The government has done this through the schools and other means. If this financial problem is occurring within two-parent households, what then is the impact to a single-parent household (divorced, widowed, or not married)?

Single-parent households make up more than 32 percent of all households in the US according the US 2000 Census. Over 75 percent of those single-parent households are headed by single moms.

This is not to say that any parent, single or married, isn't doing the best he or she can under the circumstances, but a great deal more is required. It is no wonder we are reaping broken families, youth gangs, youth crime, high teen-pregnancy rates, youth drug use, and a host of other problems. We are reaping what we have sown, the lack of discipline, morals, ethics, and spiritual guidance.

Should we be surprised that children are growing up without a proper education—an education that is not only an academic education of math, reading, history, and science, but an education of morals, spiritual and character development? Because many

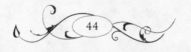

parents are absent, children are growing up without proper guidance in these areas. An education should not merely serve the purpose of earning an income; rather it should be for learning what to do with an income, after you have earned it! [8]

If we are going to relinquish our responsibility and let the government help raise our children, we should not be surprised at the outcome, because the government will not educate them properly in these areas. A child that knows how to pray, work, and think is already half-educated! [9]

How do we address this problem? There are four action steps that need to occur:

1. Families need to commit to living within their means. They must make the needed adjustments in their spending habits to accomplish this, including learning about all aspects of finances (giving, managing, and increasing). You must realize that the worst place to live is beyond one's means! [10]

2. Families need to commit to becoming and remaining debt free. Understanding that buying what you do not need is the easiest way to needing what you cannot buy! [11]

3. Parents need to take an increased and active role in their children's education and upbringing. Ecclesiasticus (Sirach) 7:23 "Have you children? Educate them; make them bow their neck from childhood." This passage commands that we teach both humility and

discipline to our children. Mastering ones' finances requires discipline.

4. Families must commit to understanding what becoming a "true" stewardship family means. My interpretation of the concept of "true" stewardship will be developed and expounded upon throughout this book using the Bible as a guideline.

This country has a major stewardship problem. Deuteronomy 15:6 speaks to giving generously; if you do, God will bless you and prosper you; you will become creditors to many nations and debtors to none. Due to extreme indebtedness of most American families, this financial principle is completely turned on its head.

We have become a nation of debtors. This bodes ill for our country and our families because debt is the slave master of the free. Did Christ purchase our freedom with his blood so that we could only enslave ourselves again with debt? Where is the wisdom in this lifestyle?

Important First Steps

I never started out thinking that there are eight steps to financial success. I studied and took many notes from Bible passages and began to categorize the passages. It became clear to me there were three principles that involved eight steps that God had placed in the Bible for me to follow. By following the eight steps, we are *guaranteed* success in *any* financial situation.

So where to start? How do you prepare yourself for this change? How do you begin to solve your problems?

Here is what I suggest you do:

•   First, if you are single (unmarried/widowed/ divorced), go to a quiet place and begin to write down *all* of your fears and problems concerning your finances. Then offer them to God. Pray to him for help. Pray to receive the seven gifts of the Holy Spirit: the gifts of wisdom, understanding, counsel, fortitude, knowledge, piety, and fear of the Lord.

If you are married, pray with your spouse, look into his or her eyes, reaffirming your love, and together write down *all* of your fears and problems concerning your finances. Then offer them to God. Together, pray to Him for help. Pray to receive the seven gifts of the Holy Spirit: the gifts of wisdom, understanding, counsel, fortitude, knowledge, piety, and fear of the Lord.

If your spouse is unwilling to participate, pray alone. Pray for healing in your marriage, pray for your spouse. Pray that your spouse's mind will open and his/her heart will soften. Never cease asking for these things!

At first these actions may seem awkward, but they will change your life forever. You must develop an intimate relationship with God. As stated before, the only way to do that is through prayer and the study of Scripture.

- Second, read and study the eight steps. Seek to master them. Devote yourself to the constant study of the Scriptures but not only the Scriptures contained in this book's pages, but throughout the Bible.

- Third and finally, seek counsel from someone who is better at finances than you. Seek someone who is deeply committed to God and has done, or is doing, what you are looking to do or who has become what you want to become.

Let us begin!

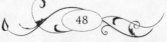

STEP #1—KEEP A WRITTEN BUDGET

I was amazed when I discovered this step. I would never have guessed that the Bible *commands* us to have a written budget. I simply never gave much thought to this before I began to really study the Scriptures. This step may have come naturally to some people, but I certainly was not one of them.

Why a Written Budget is Important

There it was in Ecclesiasticus (Sirach) 42:1–7, "These are the things you should not be ashamed of, and do not sin from fear of what others think... Whatever stores you issue, do it by number and weight, spendings and takings, *put everything in writing.*"

There it was in black and white. Keep a *written* budget! Could you ever imagine a company in today's world operating without a budget? What would that be like? The owners, officers, and employees could

not properly function. How would payroll be met and taxes be paid? Receivables and payables could not function. How could purchases be made? I seriously doubt a company could make it even a few months without operating on a budget. Yet many people do it day after day, month after month, year after year, and still do not understand why things are not working out better.

It is critical to understand this very basic step. I want to be absolutely clear: balancing a checkbook is not the same as developing a budget. Keeping track in your mind is not the same as having a budget.

"Without maintenance even the tiniest of holes will sink the mightiest of ships."

This is the simplest of all the eight steps, yet it seems to be the most difficult for people to do. Trying to live within your income is far easier than trying to live without an income! [12]

Most people think they know exactly how their money is being spent. Often, they don't realize that a few dollars spent here and a few more spent there add up to real money after some time. Without tracking where your money is going, there will be absolutely no way to ever gain control of it. If you do not gain control of it, you will never be able to change your situation.

There is a wise maritime saying that states, "Without maintenance, even the tiniest of holes will sink the mightiest of ships." Think about that for a moment. If left unchecked, financial holes will sink you. The ship maintenance is the month-to-month planning of how you spend your income.

If you do not assert control over your money, your money will certainly assert control over you. Consider Haggai 1:5–8:

> Reflect carefully how things have gone for you. You have sown much and harvested little; you eat but never have enough, drink but never have your fill, put on clothes but do not feel warm. The wage earner gets his wages only to put them into a purse that is riddled with holes.

After discovering this passage in the Old Testament, I must admit I felt a sense of shame. I was thinking I did a fairly good job at handling finances. Sure, we ended up homeless, but I thought at the time, it was due to bad luck and misfortune.

I wasn't using a written budget, but I felt I kept a good mental accounting of money. I always seemed to be several hundred dollars off, when things became tight. I could never understand how I was bouncing checks as frequently as I did. I never seemed to have as much as I thought I should.

The passage from Haggai made me realize that my problems were not the result of the amount of money I was making, or not making, but rather in how I was managing it. There are two ways to succeed financially: spend less than you make and make more than you spend. [13] The budget is the tool that helps ensure your success.

I never seemed to be financially comfortable. Now I understood why. It occurred to me, if I was

incapable of managing what little money I did have, how could I realistically expect to receive more and handle the additional money well? The analogy of the purse with holes was what really stuck with me. I could clearly picture coins (my wages) being dumped into this purse, and the coins leaking out the bottom. It would never matter if I earned $20,000 or $200,000; if the purse leaked, the result is the same. In both instances, I would be broke.

It was then that I decided we would begin to operate using a written budget. I called a meeting with my wife and announced we were going on a very strict budget. Remember, I had sold my shop and I was now working for a Fortune 200 company, in sales. Calling a meeting seemed to be how things were done in corporate America; in this case, the meeting was with my wife. My approach didn't go over so well. The mistake was that I acted as if I were the president (of our family) and that any money that would be spent, would be done, only with my approval. My wife responded something like, "Well … if I wanted your approval, I would give it to ya!" Lesson learned!

At that time I came to understand that marriage is a partnership. Both should have equal say. Yes, I was still president, but my wife was chairman of the board. We had to work at it together. I had to structure our budget to accommodate things I might not otherwise accommodate, had I not been married. We had to balance our responsibilities, needs, and wants. We had to come to an agreement on goals regarding saving, spending, and giving. We needed a balanced budget!

A Balanced Budget Reaps Rewards

Proverbs 11:1 speaks to a false balance being abhorrent to Yahweh and a just one pleasing. This proverb, although simple and straightforward, has a deeper meaning. Weights were used as they are today to measure a common agreed-upon quantity. A budget is no different than a set of scales; it measures a common quantity of income and outgo. What good is a scale if it is out of balance or short of the needed or expected quantity? God expects us to operate with a just balance—a set of scales that is honest and balanced. A budget must be both honest and balanced. Honest from a standpoint of accommodating *all* aspects of financial responsibilities and needs, and balanced so that outgo cannot, over time, financially destroy you.

These responsibilities include tithing, paying yourself, saving for retirement, and paying all debts. You must also address your needs for a place to live, food to eat, utilities, transportation, clothes, and other needs. God expects us to do this in a balanced manner. There is no possible way to be in balance, if a budget is not used.

Again, another proverb, Proverbs 13:18 states, "For the man who rejects discipline; poverty and disgrace; for the man who accepts correction: honor." The lesson here is it takes discipline to operate on a budget, but if done faithfully and correctly, honor and prosperity will be your reward; if not, you will know poverty and with that disgrace.

I can attest to this proverb's wisdom. I figured I

knew, without writing it down, where all my money was going. In my mind, I had deluded myself into thinking that I was properly budgeting. In reality, I might have done an average job at keeping track of the money, but it was *not* a budget!

What I was doing was passive management of finances. A budget is proactive management of finances. Don't be fooled into thinking that passive management is the wise way to go. By taking a passive approach to finances, you will find that your money acts more like the most unruly and belligerent of teenagers. Those of you who have experienced this phenomenon know exactly what I am talking about. Those of you who have yet to experience this, trust me, you don't want to experience it! If you are experiencing this financially, you need to focus on changing your approach. By taking a proactive approach to handling your finances, you assume *total* control of your money. You will know exactly where it goes and when. Money tends to be very obedient when handled in this manner.

Many people struggle with the idea of using a budget. They feel it is restrictive, stuffy, and takes out all of the fun and spontaneity of having money. Nothing could be further from the truth. A budget is simply a roadmap or plan of what you are going to do with your money.

You can budget for fun and spontaneity and any other activity you desire, but if your responsibilities and needs suffer, you need to adjust accordingly. If you are having financial difficulties, it is most likely

very unwise to be spontaneous with spending. A quick reference to Proverbs 17:16 would answer that objection. It states, "What good is money in a foolish hand? To purchase wisdom, when he has no sense."

I chuckled when I read this passage. I thought to myself, *Oh, how true that is!* Really, what good does money do if used foolishly? Can it buy wisdom if the possessor of it has no common sense? Money is a powerful tool when used wisely, and managed prudently.

There are three things, and three things only, to do with money:

- First, you can spend it.
- Second, you can save or invest it.
- Third, you can give it away.

I strongly believe we need to do all three; but remember, God expects us to be in balance. Let me explain!

You cannot just spend it and think you will prosper. I have yet to encounter a rich person who became rich through spending. You may acquire many things, maybe even a lot of nice things, but you will most often find yourself struggling for meaning in life or more likely a life with many money problems, including massive debt. Proverbs 21:17 cautions, "Pleasure lovers stay poor, he will not grow rich who loves wine and good living."

You cannot just save and invest it. Consider the scripture of Luke 12:13–21—the parable of avarice and greed. In this parable a wealthy man has an abun-

dant harvest come his way. He decides to tear down his barns and build bigger ones to store his blessed harvest and take life easy because he has way more than enough resources. God says to him, "You fool, tonight your life will be required of you. What then will you do with all of your possessions, to whom will they go?"

This scripture is clear in its meaning. We should focus on discovering God's purpose of why we have more than we need. We must not hoard or be greedy. We should consider those who do not have enough and give to them cheerfully and without expecting anything in return. Focusing on discovering God's purpose of your overabundance will provide your life with profound meaning.

Also, you cannot just give without providing for your own needs (spending some) and saving some for future needs, otherwise you will find yourself in dire straights as well. Ecclesiasticus (Sirach) 29:26 states, "Come to your neighbor's help as far as you can, but take care not to fall into the same plight."

Clearly, balance is needed and expected of us. A written budget is the way to wisely conduct ourselves to meet all of our responsibilities, needs, and desires in giving, saving, and spending.

Calculate Income

So how do you set up your budget? First you need to understand how much money you have coming in. The money you have coming in is your income. You will want to calculate how much you earn on a monthly basis. If you are paid semi-monthly (two times per month), or monthly (one time per month), this calculation should be very easy. If you are paid bi-weekly (every two weeks) or weekly, you will want to take what you are earning (example: $1,500 bi-weekly) and multiply that figure by 26 (number of pay-periods per year) and divide that number by 12 (twelve months). In this example, your take-home pay would be $1,500 x 26 = $39,000 annually and divide that by 12 months = $3,250/month. Weekly would be $750 x 52 (number of pay-periods in a year) and again divide by 12. Again, the take-home pay would be $3,250/month.

If you earn commissions, tips, or bonuses as part

of your income, or perhaps, that is your only source of income, you will want to average them as well. You will do this by, once again, annualizing the earnings, and arrive at a monthly average. Maybe you have great seasonal fluctuations or some other variation. No matter how you are paid, you will calculate a monthly average income. You need to include *all* income in your budget. This includes child support, structured settlements, dividends, etc.

Once you know what your average monthly income is, you will know exactly how much you have to work with. From this money you will set your tithe (10 percent).

Know Your Expenses

First things first: I often receive questions regarding tithing on gross pay (full earnings) or net pay (take-home pay after deductions). My answer is always the same. What does your heart tell you? Always keep in mind that God loves a cheerful giver. Give because you are happy to give, not because you feel obligated. Praying about this simple question will put your heart and mind at ease. In this particular example the family decides to tithe on net income.

Let's again look at the numbers. We calculated in our example above that our take-home pay was $3,250/month. After we deduct the 10 percent of tithing, we are left with $2,925 ($3,250 x 10% = $325/month in tithe). $3,250 - $325 = $2,925.

Next, pay yourself first; ideally 10 percent. $2,925 x 10% = $293 (rounded off for simplicity). $2,925 - $293 = $2,632. You now have $2,632 of income to work with for necessary expenditures and all discretionary expenses.

At this point you may be thinking to yourself, *Are you crazy?* I am struggling financially before I even begin to dive into expenses and debts. We are now looking at an additional $618 in new ones. Yes, this may *seem* crazy, but you have to follow this process to its conclusion before you judge it crazy.

Now we will examine the necessary expenses. Of these expenses, there are five categories, and only five. They are *food, housing, utilities, transportation,* and *clothing.* I have listed these categories in the order of their importance. You see, without food and water none of these other categories matter. You can live without water for about a week before you would die; food, maybe two or three months, maybe less.

A place to live (a shelter of some sort) is critical for stability, unity, and health reasons. Without a place to live, your life expectancy will be dramatically shorter. The quality of the shelter will impact to some degree your physical health. Man was created to live in some sort of shelter. People don't do well when left to the mercy of the elements.

Utilities provide comfort and are needed for a healthy lifestyle. They keep our homes warm in the winter and cool in the summer. They are essential for storage and preparation of meals, bathing and cleaning. Can you live without them? Yes, probably to some degree, but they certainly are important. That is why they are listed third.

Transportation enables us to better provide for our families. It enables us to efficiently travel to and from work. It is a great tool. Can you live without it?

Yes, but for productivity and opportunity purposes, it is extremely important, because many people live in big cities that are spread out, and to find a job that provides adequate income, it is almost a necessity.

You need to decide, is it better to find a job close to where you live, or move and live close to where you work? Understand, transportation can, and often is, an enormous expense. When you take into account car payments (sometimes more than one car), auto insurance, gas, and upkeep, you are talking about big expenses. Can you explore alternatives? Utilizing public transportation, biking, walking, working from home are all great alternatives to owning an automobile; people make these types of choices every day, and such choices can be very prudent!

Clothes are important for protection from the elements. They also provide comfort and a sense of personal modesty. In this day and age, clothes can be incredibly cheap to provide, granted you shop carefully; that is why it is listed last. Many families that are struggling make big financial mistakes by purchasing expensive designer clothes for their children and themselves. They purchase these items with great intentions, not realizing they are severely crippling their finances. Peer pressure (the pressure to fit in) and slick marketing greatly add to financial difficulties that families are experiencing. Strengthen your and your family's resolve. Your financial future may depend on not bowing to peer pressure. Remember Proverbs 21:17 (pleasure lovers stay poor)?

Now that we have identified the "big five" necessities, I want to discuss their proper costs.

✓ First, food. There is a huge opportunity to greatly control the cost of food. You have the ability to buy large amounts of healthy food for very little money. Do you eat out or buy take-out food frequently? Do you eat hamburger or steak? Do you use coupons or buy on sale or do you pay full price? A family of four should be able to live comfortably on $400/month or less. I know this can be done because I did it for a long time and with more people.

Some ideas to help keep costs down include:

- Buy as much of your food from the day-old or close-out section of your local store.

- Utilize food banks. Many communities have food banks. The food is good and cheap—often free!

- Always buy on sale and never at full price.

- Buy in bulk if it does not bust your budget. If possible, shop with friends when you do shop for bulk, so that you can split the tab. Each of you can then meet your needs, without buying more than you can use.

The cheaper you can get by on food, the more money you have to allocate elsewhere to improve your situation.

✓ Second, housing. Housing should never consume more that 33–36 percent of your gross income. That means if your gross income is $4,000/month your mortgage or rent cannot be more than $1,320-$1,440, period! The lesser the amount, the better. If you find yourself in the situation of owning or renting (home, condo, or apartment, etc.) a place that is too expensive, consider moving!

✓ Third, your utilities should never be more than 3–6 percent of your gross income. That means if your income is $4,000/month ($120-$240/month). Again, the less, the better!

Some ideas for keeping utilities costs down are:

- Turn off lights not being used

- Turn down the thermostat. If it is a programmable thermostat, it should be turned off at night and activated a half hour before the household wakes up. Use your blankets to keep warm, not the furnace!

- Keep the AC turned down or, better yet, off as much as possible.

- Wash clothes and use dishwasher late at night. Utility rates are lower during the night.

- Internet/cable/phones/cell phones are all luxuries. If you need a phone for emergencies, obtain a prepaid phone.

✓ Fourth, transportation. If you can afford a car at all, you should never own one whose value exceeds more than 50 percent of your annual income. Using our example from before, if your gross monthly income is $4,000 your gross annual income is $48,000 that means the value (or price) or your car should not exceed $24,000. If it does, you will struggle financially! If you own two cars, their combined value (price or cost) should not exceed $24,000; if they do, you must rid yourself of at least one of them and find a less expensive alternative. It does not matter what the sales person says you qualify for or can afford or what payment you have been making for a period of time before; if you do not obey this rule of thumb, you *will* sink financially!

Some ideas for keeping transportation costs down are:

- Buy used tires. Many tire shops and salvage yards sell good used tires, often at a fraction of what new ones cost.

- Learn how to do your own oil changes and basic maintenance for your vehicles. You can check out books on this subject at your local library.

It amazes me how people love their cars. Some would rather starve and drive a really nice car. What I like to stress, through example, is how cars are keeping them from being

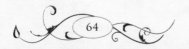

financially independent. A $300-$500 car payment month after month, year after year, is costing you more than $400,000 in future wealth. Is that good stewardship? I discuss what the effect of constant car payments has on future wealth in much greater detail in a later chapter.

✓ Fifth, and finally, clothes. Clothes should represent a very small portion of your over-all budget. If properly done, you can clothe yourself, as well as your family, for very little money. You should never have to pay full price for your clothes. Let other unwise people do that. If you want to truly change your financial future, you need to change the way you, and if you have a family, your family's way of thinking about fashion. A $100 pair of sneakers is ridiculous! I suppose if you are a multimillionaire then maybe $100 for sneakers is no big deal, but if you are struggling financially or maybe your goal is to become the best steward of God's resources that you are capable of being, and in the process becoming wealthy, then it is unwise to spend that kind of money on shoes. The fact is, I could spend a lot of time, speaking on current fashion and beauty trends, but I won't; hopefully you get the picture.

Some ideas for keeping clothes costs down are:

- Buy clothes from consignment and used clothes shops. If you are going to buy name-brand clothes, this is a great way to buy them cheaply!
- Buy clothes from ARC and thrift stores
- Buy clothes at garage sales

There is no shame in shopping in this manner. Many of the clothes are like new. No one will know the difference. You may often be surprised by meeting your neighbors who shop there too!

Again, these "big five" are what I consider necessities. You cannot completely do without them, but you can certainly exercise some control over each of these areas. You will ultimately choose how much is spent in these areas.

It is now time to discuss the discretionary expenditures of your budget. Keep in mind that everything outside of tithing, paying yourself, and the "big five" is discretionary. I define discretionary as expenditures you can live without. You will need to make some uncomfortable, and maybe even unpopular, changes in this area. I did. Some of the changes included such things as no vacations for a period of time, low spending limits on holidays and special occasions, little or no shopping trips, very limited eating out at restaurants and cutting out cable TV for a period of time. I did what I felt we had to do for the financial survival of my family.

There are sacrifices that must be made. It is important to remember that all of these cutbacks and all of these sacrifices will be temporary. Although I believe, with proper management, you should be able to enjoy an occasional night out, a family night, a date night, or other such activity. These are often what make life fun. But until your financial house is in order, it is important to entertain yourself and the family on the cheap. Examples would be checking out movies from the library, picnics in the park, free days at the zoo or other free attractions, and game nights with the family. So how do you begin your budget?

At this point, you should have your income listed. Next, you should have your tithe calculated, and the amount you are going to pay yourself. You will know how much income you will have to work with on the rest of your budget. You will then write out the "big five" in separate categories (food, housing, utilities, transportation, and clothing).

Under food you will record how much money you are currently spending on food. Under housing you will record all expenses that pertain to housing. There may be several categories under this. These may include items such as mortgage, rent, taxes, insurance, and repairs, etc. Your categories may look something like this:

Food

Groceries	$_____
Restaurant	$_____
Coffee (Starbucks)	$_____
Other	$_____
Total Food	$_____

Housing

Mortgage	$_____
Rent	$_____
Taxes	$_____

(if not already included in the mortgage payment)

Insurance	$_____

(if not already included in the mortgage payment)

Repairs/Maintenance	$_____
Improvements	$_____
Furniture Replacement	$_____
Association Fees (HOA)	$_____
Other	$_____
Total Housing	$_____

Utilities

Electricity	$_____
Gas	$_____
Water/Sewer	$_____
Phone	$_____
Cell Phone	$_____
Cable	$_____
Trash Collection	$_____
Internet	$_____
Other	$_____
Total Utilities	$_____

Transportation

Car Payment/Lease	$_____
Fuel/Oil Changes	$_____
Tires/Repair/Upkeep	$_____
Insurance	$_____
License Tags/Taxes	$_____

Replacement Fund	$_____
Other	$_____
Total Transportation	$_____

Clothes

Children	$_____
Adults	$_____
Dry Cleaning	$_____
Total Clothes	$_____

Now the discretionary spending; I would list categories such as medical, personal, recreation, and debts. Your categories may look something like this:

Medical

Health Insurance	$_____
Dental Insurance	$_____
Vision Insurance	$_____
Disability Insurance	$_____
Life Insurance	$_____
Other Insurance	$_____
Doctor	$_____
Dentist	$_____
Eye Glasses	$_____
Orthodontia	$_____
Prescriptions	$_____
Other	$_____
Total Medical	$_____

A note on the medical section: Some people inquire about this being more important than, say, clothes. I have come to believe the wiser you are, the more important health and other insurances (den-

tal, life, and disability to mention a few) become. Understand, you need clothes; new ones, old ones, it doesn't matter, but you need clothes! You can live without medical insurance for a while; it can be very unwise to do so for an extended period of time. I am a living example of that. You will need to judge your personal situation.

Personally, I would make sure to adequately fund this part of your budget, even if you have to take on a part-time job to afford it. If you or your family have medical needs, then it makes complete sense to make sure your budget adequately addresses it. You do not want to end up in a situation such as mine was, if you are already struggling. The thing about health and medical insurance is that there will always be a question of when you need it. If you need it, and you don't have the insurance, it is already too late.

Many times insurance can be provided through your work. You may not have to budget for it because it is already being deducted from your pay. Remember, we are talking about take-home pay for budget purposes. You will still have to budget for things like co-pays and prescriptions. Now let's get back to the discretionary spending items.

Personal

Child Care	$_____
Cleaning Products	$_____
Toiletries	$_____
Education	$_____
School Tuition	$_____
School Supplies	$_____

Cosmetics	$_____
Child Support	$_____
Alimony	$_____
Subscriptions	$_____
Gifts	$_____
Christmas	$_____
Dues	$_____
Misc.	$_____
Crazy Money	$_____
Other	$_____
Personal Total	$_____

Notes or ideas on some of the aforementioned items:

- Cleaning products—These products should never be purchased from the grocery store. They are very expensive. They can be bought at stores such as Savers, Big Lots, and $.99 stores for a fraction of the cost.

- School supplies—These items can also be bought at discount stores and $.99 stores. You do not have to buy a year's supply of paper and pencils at one time.

- Christmas (or any other special occasion time)—It is best to budget for these type of items on a monthly basis. If you are budgeting $600 for Christmas, you should set aside $50 each month starting in January. By the time Christmas rolls around, you have $600 without destroying your budget ($50 x 12 months = $600). Position your finances to take advan-

tage of "crazy-type" sales (after-Thanksgiving sales). Be prepared!

Recreation

Entertainment	$_____
Special Occasion	$_____
Vacation	$_____
Sports/Activities	$_____
Other	$_____
Recreation Total	$_____

Sub-totals Expenses

Food	$_____
Housing	$_____
Utilities	$_____
Transportation	$_____
Clothing	$_____
Medical	$_____
Personal	$_____
Recreation	$_____
Total of All Expenses	$_____

If your budget shows you are spending more than you are bringing in, congratulations, you have identified your problem. You then must go back and begin hacking, cutting, and trimming until it is in the positive. The more positive you can make it, the better. Once you have done this, you are on the road to success. Do not forget, we still must deal with the debt you have.

Starting a new month with a budget in place is an incredibly powerful position. Don't forget balance. Celebrate *all* of your wins, in an appropriate and prudent manner.

The discussion on debt and how it is budgeted for will be discussed in the future chapter of Step #4 "Eliminate Debt Until Only the Mortgage Remains."

Teach Your Children about Budgeting

What we teach our children about budgets and budgeting will impact their lives forever. Are you teaching them the importance of understanding the power that a financial plan (a budget) provides? Are you teaching them what to do with their money after they have earned it? Most everyone knows how to earn money—but not one in one thousand knows how to wisely spend it. Educating them on the use of this powerful tool, *the budget,* will teach them how to make better choices in the allocation of their money. Some ideas to help children learn about budgeting are:

1. Children love to accompany their parents to the supermarket. Have them compose a list of items that you need. Ask them to write down how much they think each item might cost (feel free to help them if they struggle with this), then add up the items and project how much will be spent. Find coupons (if you

have them) and use them. Stick as close to the projected amount on the list as possible. Have them hunt (comparison shop) for the items on the list. Make a game of it.

2. When your children are given or earn money, have them create wish lists of how they would like to spend it. You must remind them to give a portion away and save a portion of their money. The remainder should be used towards responsibilities or obtaining the items on their wish list.

You are missing an incredible life-lesson opportunity if you are not passing on the wisdom of operating from a "balanced" financial plan. Children need to understand that there are three things and three things only that a person can do with money. You can save it, you can spend it, or you can give it away. God expects you to do all three—in balance. You should save at least 10 percent or $.10 for each dollar earned for a "rainy" day. You should give away (tithe) at least 10 percent or $.10 for each dollar back to God and the poor of the world. The remaining 80 percent is for responsibilities and enjoyment.

Having children plan how they will allocate their earned money will be a lesson they will never forget. Having them assist with the family budget is a life lesson that will come to serve them well when they are grown and on their own. They will have become accustomed to the discipline needed to operate from a written budget.

Written Budget—In Review

It is critical to create and operate from a written budget. Your priority must be to enter each month with a balanced budget (a budget that accommodates *all* aspects of money—giving, spending, and saving). If you have a shortfall of income in any given month, you must cut back in your discretionary spending for that month. Do not spend money you have not allocated or earned!

Scriptures to live by:

Ecclesiasticus (Sirach) 42:1–7 (a written budget)

Haggai 1:5–8 (fixing your money leaks)

Proverbs 11:1 (a balanced budget—balance in spending/saving and investing/giving)

STEP #2—TITHING

Why Tithe?

Why is tithing important? It is important to remember that we should give according to our income(s), lest God make our income(s) according to our giving.[14] I did not fully understand the importance of tithing until I discovered in the Bible all of the implications of tithing. I wanted to truly understand it. Where did this concept come from? Why 10 percent? Does it apply to Christians today? Why is tithing important? Does it mean that it all should be given to the church?

The first mention of tithing in scripture is to be found in Genesis 14:20, which states, "Blessed be Abram by God Most High, creator of heaven and earth, and blessed be God Most High for handing over your enemies to you. And Abram gave a tithe of everything."

This passage from Genesis mentions tithing around 1850 BC, but there is no way to know when tithing actually began. Genesis 26:12–14 describes Jacob as

making a vow that if God delivered him safely on his journey that he would tithe to God. It states:

> Jacob made this vow, "If God goes with me and keeps me safe on this journey I am making, if he gives me bread to eat and clothes to wear, and if I return home safely to my father, then Yahweh shall be my God. This stone I have set up as a monument shall be a house of God, and I will surely pay you a tenth part of all you give me."

Jacob began his journey with nothing more than the clothes on his back and a walking staff but returned many years later a very wealthy man. In most all accounts in the Bible, tithing is tied to prosperity in all of its facets. Leviticus 27:30 summarized that all first fruits of labor and produce of the land belong to God.

Mosaic Law (Jewish Law) required that tithes be paid. They were obligatory. Hebrews (Jews) had three tithes they were commanded to follow. The first was the annual tithe in which each year everyone was required to give a tenth of all their herd or flock, a tenth of all the produce of the land, and they were to give it to whatever place Yahweh chose to make a home for his name—a temple (a church). People were commanded to not neglect "the Levite" (the priestly class) who lived in the towns.

"I will surely pay you a tenth of all you give me." Genesis 26:14

The second tithe was the third-year tithe. Every third year a tithe was commanded to be given to "the Levites," the stranger, the orphan, and the widow so

that they may live and be cared for. Again, Deuteronomy 14:29 cites that if this is done, that God will bless you in all of the work your hands undertake.

The third tithe was known as the sabbatical year. This tithe occurred every seven years. The Hebrews were commanded to grant a remission on all debts of brothers (family and other Hebrews). They were not to exact payment from each other on debts during this year. They were commanded to share with each other so that their needs were met and that they may be blessed in all of their endeavors. Again, God made a very powerful promise of prosperity. He promised if these laws were followed, that, "You would become creditors to many nations and debtors to none" (Deuteronomy 15:6).

So what is the significance of 10 percent? It is not known exactly why 10 percent, but ten had always been considered a complete number. There are only ten numbers in our number system. Every other number is derived from the first ten numbers. Ten signified totality, a concept that could easily be associated with God. Tithing was done as a way of learning fear of the Lord. Not fear in the sense of being afraid, but rather, a complete respect for God's sovereignty—the innate understanding that God owns everything. Consider Psalm 50:8–11, it reads:

> "I am not finding fault with your sacrifices, those holocausts constantly before me; I do not claim one extra bull from your home nor one extra goat from your pens, 'since all the forest animals are already mine, and the cattle on my mountains in

their thousands; I know all the birds of the air, nothing moves in the field that does not belong to me."

We are merely stewards of God's resources.

Many people question whether the Old Testament concept of tithing applies to Christians today. Careful study and contemplation of Scripture would reveal a resounding "yes!" Jesus himself said that he came to fulfill the law, not destroy it. "Do not imagine that I have come to abolish the Law or the Prophets. I have come not to abolish but to complete them" (Matthew 5:17).

The prophet Isaiah foretold of a suffering servant almost 740 years before Christ appeared. The Old Testament book of Isaiah is filled with prophecies that Christ fulfilled. In Isaiah 53:4–5, there is described a suffering servant in what we as Christians recognize as Christ. It states:

> And yet ours were the sufferings he bore, ours the sorrows he carried. But we thought of him as someone punished, struck by God and brought low. Yet he was pierced through our own faults, crushed for our sins. On him lies a punishment that brings us peace, and through his wounds we are healed.

Another reference would be Isaiah 42:6–7, which states, "I have appointed you … To open the eyes of the blind, to free captives from prison, and those who live in darkness from the dungeon."

Clearly there are many passages that speak of a Messiah, a tortured servant, whom we Christians

believe to be Christ, as being the fulfillment of the covenant. There is a saying that goes, "the New Testament lies hidden in the Old, and the Old Testament is unveiled in the New." Christ came so that the blind would see and to raise the standards, not dispel or disband them. Christians are held to a higher standard than everyone else.

Financially speaking, we are held to the highest of standards. We are called to give and give generously. Why should we as Christians, who are not obligated under Mosaic Law to give 10 percent, give any less than someone who is under Mosaic Law? 2 Corinthians 9:6–9 reads:

> Do not forget thin sowing means thin reaping; the more you sow the more you reap. Each one of you should give what he has decided in his own mind, not grudgingly or because he is made to, for *God loves a cheerful giver.* And there is no limit to the blessings which God can send you—he will make sure that you always have all that you need for yourselves in every possible circumstance, and still have something to spare for all sorts of good works.

I believe the key in the last scripture is "what he has decided in his own mind, not grudgingly or because he is made to, for *God loves a cheerful giver.*" The Bible directs us to make a decision on tithing; either we decide to tithe, or we decide not to tithe. We should tithe because we want to, not because we are obligated. Many people do not sit down and plan what their contribution at Sunday mass will be.

Would you leave on a trip without giving any thought as to how much money would be required to complete it? Many people take more time to plan their spending for their trip than they spend planning their giving. Many people toss a few bucks into the collection basket without contemplating the significance of their gift. "Thin sowing means thin reaping."

God never intended tithing to be easy. It is "sacrificial" in nature. What is the meaning of tithing if it is done from only what remains? There is nothing sacrificial about giving from your leftovers. If there is nothing left over, then you do not or cannot tithe. Most people mistakenly think and act on tithing from this perspective. This is the reason very few people tithe. Tithing before you have spent your income requires sacrifice. It forces you to live off the remaining 90 percent of your income. This may be difficult for most people. In addition, tithing can be one of the most difficult steps to comprehend and accomplish because it involves a *leap of faith*. When I counsel people on this process, the very first thought that comes to their minds is, *I would love to tithe, but how can I expect to give 10 percent of my income when I don't even have enough income to pay my bills?*

The answer is simple: because you are really tithing right now! The right question is: to which god? The one true God or the god of mammon (the god of Citibank, the god of Ford Motor Credit, the god of Exxon-Mobil, the god of Starbucks Coffee, the god of Wal-Mart, and even the god of McDonald's)?

If you were to pause now and seriously ponder that question, what would your reply be? If it is not to the one true God, are you going to continue making the choice of tithing to the god of mammon?

Thorough study of the Scriptures leads to an absolutely clear mandate from God (in the Old Testament), reinforced with Jesus' teachings about giving (tithing) in the New Testament. For instance, the Old Testament prophet Malachi states in 3:8–11:

> Can a man cheat God? Yet you are cheating me. You ask, "How are we cheating you?" In the matter of tithes and dues. The curse lies on you because you, yes you the whole nation, are cheating me. Bring the full tithes and dues to the storehouse so that there may be food in my house, and then see if I do not open the floodgates of heaven and pour out a blessing for you in abundance.

Clearly this says that if I am not tithing first fruits (10 percent of my income), that I am cheating God. Can you honestly think that there will be no consequences to cheating God?

Does this mean that I am being forced to tithe? Of course not, but I believe that God clearly wants us to trust him completely for everything. He promises that if we do give (tithe), we will be blessed abundantly.

Luke 6:46–49 refers to "the true disciple" stating:

> "Why do you call me 'Lord, Lord' and not do what I say? Everyone who comes to me and listens to my words and acts on them—I will show you what he is like. He is like the man who when

he builds his house dug and dug deep, and laid his foundations on rock; when the river was in flood it bore down on that house but could not shake it, it was so well built. But the one who listens and does nothing is like the man who built his house on soil, with no foundations: as soon the river bore down on it, it collapsed; and what a ruin that house became!"

Christ asks us to listen to his words and act on them. He commands us to love one another, help one another, and he asks us to give, and give generously to any in need, so that our foundations will be built on rock, and will withstand, through his Father's blessing, any flood.

1 Timothy 6:17–19 reads:

Warn those who are rich in the world's goods that they are not to look down on other people; and not to set their hopes on money, which is untrustworthy, but on God who, out of his riches, gives us all that we need for our happiness. Tell them they are to do good, and be rich in good works, to be generous and willing to share. This is the way they can save up a good capital sum for the future if they want to make sure of the only life that is real.

People want to know if all of their tithe should go to the church. My reply is always the same. You must pray and let God direct your heart on this subject. A scripture that, in my opinion, answers this question directly is Deuteronomy 14:22–23. It says, "Every year you must take a tithe of all that your sowing yields on the land and in the presence of Yahweh your God, in the place he chooses to give his name a home ... so shall you learn to fear Yahweh your God always."

This passage states what God expects of our offering (our tithe). He asks that it be given to the place he chooses to give his name a home—his church! My belief is that you are expected to support the place from whence you draw your spiritual nourishment. If, however, you feel God is directing you to help outside his church, by all means, follow his direction.

It wasn't until I decided to tithe that my financial situation began to change. I had no idea how my situation would work, because I was so in debt and had very little money. Most of the time I felt like I had not even made it through the first week of the month and all of the money had been spent. I had to keep reminding myself about overcoming my debt with the saying, "The best way to eat an elephant is one bite at a time." What I struggled with was how I would eat the rest of the herd.

It was not until I had followed step #1 (a written budget) that I first began to see the possibility of where the 10 percent would come from. I began to see that I was tithing already; although it wasn't to the correct god. Without following step #1, I would never have discovered this fact. I had a number of financial leaks. I did have more money than I thought. I just did not have complete control over what I had. Once I firmly understood my financial situation, tithing became a matter of priority. Prior to that, tithing had not been a consideration. When I began to focus on giving 10 percent, I was forced into a more disciplined spending of the remaining 90 percent.

The more Old and New Testament Scriptures I discovered pertaining to finances, the more I was convinced that giving (tithing) was needed in order to truly prosper. Mark 4:24–25 read, "He also said to them, Take notice of what you are hearing. The amount you measure out is the amount you will be given—and more besides; for the man who has will be given more; from the man who has not, even what he has will be taken away."

What I realized was that what I was giving (little or nothing), was being given back to me as little or nothing. It was painfully obvious, what little I had, was being taken from me in various ways; mostly by the IRS, bill collectors, or attorneys representing bill collectors.

I was living Mark 4:24–25. I was learning a tough divine principle, the principle of "sowing and reaping." God was speaking to me. I knew I needed to change. This was a very humbling lesson.

Another compelling scripture pertaining to tithing, or more accurately not tithing, is Haggai 1:7–10. The consequences are predictable. It reads:

> Reflect carefully how things have gone for you. The abundance you expected proved to be little. When you brought in the harvest my breath spoiled it. While my house lies in ruins you are busy with your own, each one of you. That is why the sky has withheld the rain and the earth its yield.

This is an incredibly powerful scripture about tithing and giving in general. God plainly says that the reason you have not prospered is because you are worried about your own house, your own affairs, and your own problems. Understand, some people put "nothing" in the church collection and yet complain that the church is too cold! [15]

God's kingdom lies in ruin, and his people in depravation, because we are too focused on ourselves. He asks that we take care of his people and his kingdom. If we do this, he says he will pour out blessings in abundance. Remember the scripture of 2 Corinthians 9:6–9? It spoke of giving generously because God loves a cheerful giver, and there is no limit to the blessings that God will send you. He will make sure you have more than enough in all instances.

Another passage that speaks to this is Luke 6:36–38. It says if you give, you will be given in return "a full measure pressed down, shaken together and will be poured into your lap."

I have no difficulty in picturing this passage. I could imagine a measuring cup being filled with a full gallon of milk. The cup would be filled to the brim quickly and soon would overflow. I would quickly try to contain the spill but would be unable to do so. This is an incredibly vivid picture of what God's promise is about. Tithing is the basis of all giving.

Has it always been easy since I began tithing? Of course not! I have had a number of financial challenges along the way. God never promised you won't have challenges, but he has promised that you will

prosper. I believe God will place challenges or difficulties (remember James 1:2–4?), even great difficulties, in our lives to aid in our growth and maturation as Christians.

In the end, I must have faith that God knows, far better than I, what needs to be done in order to prosper. I must admit I have prospered since I began tithing (we obtained our dream home). I feel my marriage is more blessed. I feel my family is more blessed. I feel all of my work and grand projects are blessed.

I have often been asked by many people, as well as my parents, "If you could change what happened; if you could change all of the trials and tribulations including being homeless, would you?" My answer is always a resounding *no!*

I would never want to change what I have experienced in the last fifteen years. If I were to do that, I would most certainly not be the person I am today. I would not be where I am today. I would definitely not have what I have today. God empowered me to understand his plan for me and changed my heart toward giving. His grace and love have brought all of the blessings I enjoy today.

When should tithing start? The best time to start is now! The person who procrastinates will struggle with ruin. [16] The worse your situation, the quicker you should heed this sound biblical advice. Understand, you may have no idea how tithing will work in your budget. I understand your doubt, I myself had doubt. That is why it may be a very good idea that you seek counsel. There are small differences in people's situations that can make a big impact when figuring out how to make tithing work.

I have often posed a challenge to people that I counsel who are having financial difficulties and who give very little to their church, to start tithing. Once we have walked through the numbers, every one of them had more money than they originally thought.

Now that you see the numbers contained within your budget, are you prepared to accept the challenge involved with tithing? Commit to tithe for six months (the full 10 percent). After six months, if your finances are not noticeably better, if you feel you have been more generous to God than God has been generous to you, then stop tithing. If, however, you discover that your financial situation has improved, continue tithing. My experience has proven that God is most generous.

How often in your life have you been promised something that you have absolutely no doubt would be fulfilled? God keeps *all* of his promises! God's promise is so certain, that I have no fear whatever that tithing works.

Ecclesiasticus (Sirach) 29:15 "Deposit generosity in your storerooms and it will release you from every misfortune."

Are you willing to take the challenge?

What Your Children Need to Know about Tithing

Teaching our children to tithe is critical to financial character development. Learning to give is the cornerstone to achieving true wealth. Your children will learn to think of God before self. This proper attitude will provide blessings to them throughout their lives.

Contemporary society teaches instant gratification. Society also teaches: if it feels good, do it! Teaching your children that there is more joy in giving, than receiving, will ensure that they have the proper attitude to handle wealth. Let your children see you give. Explain to them why God wants you to give. Explain what giving does for the receiver, and just as importantly, for the giver. Encourage them to give at least 10 percent or $.10 for each dollar they earn. God promises to bless the giver.

Tithing—In Review

Tithing must be seen as the foundation for creating wealth. No financial house can be solid without a solid foundation. If we expect to prosper, we must learn to give, and give freely. We must understand that *nothing* we have belongs to us—our house, our belongings, and especially our money. It all belongs to God!

Scriptures to live by:

2 Corinthians 9:6–9 (Give generously, God loves a cheerful giver.)

Luke 6:36–38 (Give and you will be given in return.)

Haggai 1:7–10 (Reflect how things have gone for you, God's house lies in ruins while you are

worried about your own problems. That is
why you are not blessed.)

Luke 6:46–49 (Why do you call out to the Lord
and not do what he says?)

Malachi 3:8–11 (Are you cheating God with your
giving? Give and see if he does not bless you
in abundance.)

Deuteronomy 14:22–23 (Deposit your tithe in
the place God has decided to give his name a
home—his church.)

STEP #3—PAY YOURSELF FIRST/ESTABLISH AN EMERGENCY FUND

Paying Yourself First—Pays off!

A secret to financial success is to spend what you have left after saving, instead of saving what is left over after spending! [17]

I was taken aback when I discovered the Bible instructs us to set aside savings. I think most people understand and would agree with the general concept of having some savings for emergencies, but to actually discover that the Bible speaks to this very issue takes most by complete surprise. Most people do not have proper emergency funds. The emergency fund(s), if they actually exist, are usually the first to go when people experience a tough spot financially, even though an emergency has not occurred. That is the single reason it is so difficult to recover from financial distress.

The Bible instructs us to pay ourselves a portion

of everything we earn after we have offered our tithe.
Proverbs 6:6–11 states:

> Idler go to the ant, ponder her ways, and grow
> wise: no one gives her orders, no overseer, no mas-
> ter, yet all through the summer she makes sure
> of her food, and gathers her supplies at harvest
> time. How long do you intend to lie there, idler?
> When are you going to rise from your sleep? A
> little sleep, a little drowsiness, a little folding of
> the arms to take life easier, and like a vagrant,
> poverty is at your elbow and, like a beggar, want.

Wow! After reading this passage, I felt like what
Goliath must have felt after being struck in the fore-
head by David's stone. I didn't die, of course, but the
sharpness of the lesson left
me awestruck! I pondered
for a while the words I had
just read. I thought, *What
a great way to teach a divine
principle.* An ant, one of the smallest of God's creatures, taught me a financial principle that completely
changes my financial situation.

*"You will pay
yourself a fair share of
everything you earn."*

What I learned from the ant was, without an
overseer, the ant diligently collects her supplies during the time of plenty and saved a portion of all that
she had collected, so that when winter came she
had enough to survive. An ant had more sense than
I did! I wasn't saving a portion of anything I was
earning, for the financial winters to come. The lesson
with which I had to come to grips was not whether
a financial winter would arrive, but when! That was

something I could now completely relate to. Living in Colorado, I have no memory of a time when winter never came. That, of course, is because winter always came. It always came, at some point, after fall. So if it can always be counted upon that winter comes after fall, is it such a stretch to believe that you will never at some point, experience a financial winter? Does it not make sense to always be prepared for a financial winter?

The part about the idler, I can relate to also. After each financial crisis I felt, *Whew! I made it through that, now I can relax a little.* It never seemed very long before the next crisis would rear its ugly head. Continuing in this cycle, I definitely found myself in poverty and in great want. *We ended up homeless!*

So what does it mean "to pay yourself first"? It means following step #1 creating a "written" budget. After you have created your budget, you will know what your situation really is. You will then proceed to step #2. You will tithe back to God what is rightfully his, 10 percent! From the remaining 90 percent of your total earnings, you will pay yourself a fair share of everything you earn (ideally 10 percent), before paying toward any debts you may have.

A better way to think of this may be the following analogy: Your financial situation is like a shovel, and your debt and bills are the hole. People often think that by continuing to dig, somehow they will get out of a hole. The only thing that happens is the hole gets bigger and deeper. Sometimes the shovel and hole seem to take on lives of their own. The shovel

keeps digging, and the hole gets bigger as you are doing nothing but watching. "Paying yourself first" is like a ladder; every time you pay yourself first, your ladder adds steps. Finally, after some time, you have enough steps to climb out of the hole. This is the best way to begin the process of changing your financial situation.

This may sound like a difficult way because your situation is so dire, but remember the ant, ponder her ways, and grow wise. The first comment(s) I usually receive from someone I am counseling through these steps are, "Okay, I am having financial difficulty now. You want me to take 10 percent and begin tithing?"

"Yes!"

"Okay, I get that. Now you want me to take yet more and pay myself before I pay my bills?"

"Yes! That is the process."

"I don't have enough to pay my bills now, and you want me to give 10 percent in a tithe and then another 10 percent (ideally) to myself?"

"Yes!" Let me explain how this works. I can't spend much time on the first 10 percent (the tithing) because if you have not grasped that, at this point, you need to put a bookmark in this chapter and go back to re-read the chapter on tithing.

The second 10 percent can be very intimidating at first, but please bear with me. You will want to construct your budget to accommodate this amount. You need to be less worried about what your creditors think and more worried about yourself, and if you have a family, about them. Any creditor will understand the principle of "paying yourself first," if you explain what you are doing (you will communicate to *all* of your creditors regularly and provide them a copy of your budget). They may gripe and threaten you, but they will accept it! If you do not ponder the ant's ways and grow wise, you will never change your financial situation.

People often challenge me with "What if I am behind and they are threatening me? Creditors continually hound me to pay off the account or demand that I pay a certain amount, and I have to. I have no choice." The truth is they are limited with what they can say to you. They can never be abusive, they can say they will sue you, and they may very well try that, but if you aren't paying now, what will a lawsuit accomplish? They will incur costs in doing it and unless you are bouncing checks, they cannot make you pay more than you owe. That is the law!

I want you to take a minute and really think about what you have just read. I experienced the same scenario when I was in such miserable financial shape. I received calls several times a day, "This is so-and-so, from so-and-so, representing so-and-so. We are attempting to collect a debt. You owe us such-and-such, and I must tell you that if you do not pay the full amount right now you will have a lot more to pay." Hearing this really scared me. I would whip out my checkbook and write a check on the spot.

The frightening part was that now our rent had been spent. We had no money for food. The electricity to my store would be shut off in the next few days

because I was so behind. I was planning on using the money for those important things, and now it was spent. Yes, I paid off a debt, but now I had new problems. I had paid this debt in a moment of panic. I had *zero* control over the money and the situation. You will *never* win if you find yourself in such a situation.

No matter what your situation is, what you need to do is to create a budget, of which you will provide a copy to all of your creditors. You then tithe and pay yourself first. Then, and only then, you worry about the creditors, period! You have now begun to assert control over both your money and your situation. When you get the calls—and you will—don't worry, you don't have to talk to any of them. You can tell them you will include them on the list to receive your financial plan. Believe it or not, most all creditors will work with you when you take this approach. The ones that feel they can do and act (uncooperatively and ruthlessly) any way they want, can be dealt with another way. You can request that they no longer contact you (often, this will need to be done in writing). This piece of advice is well worth the effort. We will discuss working with creditors more in the next chapter (Step #4—Eliminating Debt Until Only the Mortgage Remains). Let's talk about the budget numbers of paying yourself first.

To make the numbers work, you may need to decrease the amount you are currently sending your creditors. As stated before, you must communicate to them what your plan is, by providing them a copy of your written budget. You will agree to pay them a certain amount (whatever that amount may be) every month on a timely basis. You will communicate with them frequently, letting them know if your situation changes for the better or worse. For instance, if you receive overtime and have more money in your budget for that month, you will send an additional amount to your creditors. If, for instance, you have less work in a month and therefore less money in your budget, you will send less to your creditors for that month.

Continue paying yourself first until you have a substantial amount of reserves, at least $1,500. The amount needs to be sufficient to deal with any financial emergency (financial winter) that may occur. You need to look at your personal situation and make a decision. For some people, that might be $5,000. You need to look at things like: What if we have the car problems? What if the water heater or furnace fails? What if we had a big medical bill? I'm not talking about a heart transplant or cancer and you have no insurance; I am talking about a trip to the emergency room.

Once you have saved the amount determined necessary to protect yourself from an impending financial emergency, you will cease paying yourself that amount. You will then apply the "pay yourself first" money to your creditors. This process will be discussed in more detail in the next chapter. If you have an emergency and need to utilize the emergency

funds, do so, but you will revert back to "pay yourself first" until your reserves have been replenished.

I have counseled many people through difficult situations using this principle. Proverbs 10:5 says, "Gathering in the summer is the mark of the prudent, sleeping at harvest is the sign of the shameless." What this says regarding finances is the need to save a portion of what is earned in times of plenty (summertime), so that there are needed resources when there is a time of scarcity (winter); to act any other way is shameful.

A powerful message is to be found in James 4:17. It states, "Everyone who knows what the right thing to do and doesn't do it commits a sin." Now that you know what you should be doing financially, are you going to sin by not doing it?

What is needed now is a moment to discuss emergencies. You need to have a very firm idea of what constitutes an emergency. Having a birthday party at Chuck E. Cheese's for one of your children is not an emergency. Christmas or birthday presents for the family or others are not an emergency. A summer vacation to get away is not an emergency. Changing the paint or wallpaper in the bathroom is not an emergency. Paying a cell phone bill that is overdue is not an emergency. Hopefully, you are getting a clear picture of where this is heading. You do *not* use this money for non-emergency purposes. If unsure of what constitutes an emergency, feel free to seek counsel with people whom you respect and get his/her and maybe even others' opinions.

If you are sincere in wanting to change your financial picture, it is critical to faithfully practice "paying yourself first"! Proverbs 24:3–4 reads, "By wisdom a house is built, by discernment the foundation is laid; by knowledge its storerooms filled with riches of every kind rare and desirable."

If you picture your finances as a house being constructed, how would you begin? How would the process look? The previous passage clearly states, "By wisdom it is built." Consider the ant once again, ponder her ways, and gain wisdom.

In the construction of a house, one of the first processes that must occur is laying the foundation. When constructing the foundation, the builder must take into account such things as how deep the foundation must go to accommodate freezing temperatures and the types of soils that surround the house (are they expanding soils). What many people do not know is that the foundation itself has a support called a "footing." The footing prevents the foundation from sinking into the soil. It provides strength and stability. No house can be properly constructed without proper footings. If you have ever dealt with a house that has a foundation problem, you know that they are very difficult to repair and very expensive. So by paying yourself first, creating a pool of reserve money (a footing) is truly a wise thing to do to strengthen your financial foundation. By discernment (your decisions), you will pay yourself first to strengthen your foundation. Operating in this manner consistently will enable you to finish your finan-

cial house and fill your storerooms with many wonderful things.

Now is the time to take a moment and discuss stewardship in a very broad sense. There are three key principles to financial stewardship. I mentioned them at the very beginning of this book.

The first is "giving," the second is "managing," and the third is "increase." As I said before, these principles were deeply intertwined with the eight steps. Paying yourself first is part of mastering the "management" principle of financial stewardship. Do not believe, without first mastering "giving," that it is possible to truly be successful at "managing," and without mastering "managing," there will be no way to truly experience "increase."

I have discovered that there is a very logical progression to these *divine principles*. To experience success, you must adhere to these principles. Wisdom is gained when you realize that methods and practices change all the time, but principles do not! Principles are foundational. One must adhere to them at all times. They are part of the foundation of your financial house.

Once you have accomplished this step, that of "paying yourself first/establish an emergency fund," move on to step #4. Mastering "pay yourself first" will change your life!

What Your Children Need to Know about Paying Themselves First

Are you teaching your children this very important step? Are you teaching them that after tithing, paying themselves first is most important? This will help them develop the needed discipline to build long-term wealth. This will then train them to spend less than what they earn. By faithfully practicing this principle, they will build a reservoir of surplus money for an emergency life sends their way. Teach them to be diligent, like one of God's most diligent creatures, the ant. Teach them the wisdom of setting aside a portion of everything they earn for the financial winters of the future.

Teaching your children how to build long-term wealth will change their lives forever. The practice of paying themselves first will condition their character to be better stewards. It will better prepare them to properly handle wealth that you may pass onto them.

Pay Yourself First—In Review

Paying yourself first is essential in turning around a poor or struggling financial situation. Even if your current financial situation is good, paying yourself first is a wise thing to do. It is the safety-line that prevents the creation of new debt, because it is never a matter of if, but rather a matter of when, a financial winter will appear! Will you be ready?

Scriptures to live by:

Proverbs 6:6–11 (Remember the ant and grow wise. Prepare by saving a small portion of everything you make.)

Proverbs 10:5 (Gathering—setting aside portions of your harvest (income), is a wise thing to do.)

James 4:17 (If you know what you are supposed to be doing and don't do it, you are committing a sin.)

Proverbs 24:3–4 (Wisdom is critical to building a strong financial foundation.)

STEP #4—ELIMINATE DEBT UNTIL ONLY THE MORTGAGE REMAINS

What Is Your Attitude Toward Debt?

This is my favorite step. Why? Because, since my financial woes began, I felt good about myself for the first time. I had a plan and could actually see progress being made. My herd of elephants was still a herd, but it was a herd, minus one elephant's leg.

My dedication to the study of scripture led me to conclude I was on the right track with my attitude. It was this study that kept me on track. A proper attitude toward money is much more important than knowledge about money. You could know everything about money and still be a financial train wreck because of problems with attitudes. It is significantly more difficult to fail financially, if you have a proper attitude. A proper attitude toward money is that you *despise* debt.

The Bible does not speak well of debt with the

exception of Romans 13:8–9, which reads: "Avoid getting into debt, except the debt of mutual love. If you love your fellow man you have carried out your obligation."

Oddly, nowhere else in the Bible, that I have found, does it say anything good about debt. To the contrary, everything says avoid, avoid, avoid! Do not go into debt. There must be something to this!

I remember heading home one day from my shop. I needed to stop by the bank to deposit money. The bank branch that I used was in an affluent neigh-borhood. I would drive by and wonder what people did for a living that they could afford such big and beautiful houses. Were they all doctors, lawyers, and stockbrokers? Most of these homes had to be $600,000-$1,000,000 or more in 1996. I had no idea how someone could earn the kind of money needed to afford them. We were living in a rental house. At the time I was struggling to meet my rent payment of $1,050 each month; only a year earlier we were homeless because we couldn't even afford $395 each month for rent. I thought to myself, *I need to find out what these people do, and start doing some of that!*

> "A proper attitude toward money is that you despise debt."

I had delinquent rent payments, delinquent car payments, delinquent credit card payments, delin-quent student loan payments, delinquent loan pay-ments, delinquent finance company payments, delin-quent utility payments, delinquent federal, state, and local tax payments, and lots and lots of delin-quent medical debt. My life was one whole major delinquency.

Whenever I had the chance, I would talk to people (those that owned those gorgeous homes). I would inquire as to what they did. How did they get there? What were their biggest challenges? To my surprise, many of them were not what I would con-sider to be wealthy. Most had enormous amounts of debt. Some had been very wealthy and lost it sud-denly by some stroke of fate. They lived their life-style much the same way I had lived mine, except on a grander scale. They made lots of money, and they spent it all. Some of them had less money than I did. They were living off credit. I learned a lot from hav-ing these discussions. Most were very nice people, but they too, had problems.

The scripture of Haggai kept running through my mind; the one about having a purse riddled with holes. I wanted so badly to be free of financial worry. I wanted a vehicle that worked, chicken instead of beans, not to have fear about who was calling when the phone rang, and have a sense of peace that when I opened a bill, I could feel good about paying it on time. I understood that what I was doing was work-ing. I needed to stay on track.

I talked to people whom I thought were wealthy. I compared what they told me and what I knew Scrip-ture said. I loved speaking to people who were in line with scripture. They knew it and they professed it. I

paid close attention to them. I asked them a lot of questions.

I learned two points about creating wealth and being wealthy. The first was, it is far less important how much money a person earns than how it is used. You will be just as broke if you earn $40,000 or $400,000, if you spend it all! Of course most people would agree that earning $400,000 is better than earning $40,000, but it has to be used wisely. The second point in creating wealth was about how much you saved and invested. A person that earns $400,000 a year and spends $400,000 a year is going to be far less wealthy than a person who earns $40,000 each year but saves $5,000 of it. Yes, the person who earns $400,000 earns a lot of money and probably has many nice things, like a big house in a very upscale neighborhood, they probably drive a nice car and take exotic vacations, but if they spend everything they make, they will *never* become wealthy. Wealth has to do with net worth, not net pay. Proverbs 13:11 states: "A sudden fortune will dwindle away, he who grows rich who accumulates little by little."

The lesson learned from this was if I could earn $40,000 and save even $2,000, I would someday become wealthy. I wanted to fully understand God's financial plan for me. How can you participate in God's plan if you are enslaved by debt? You may be thinking, *Why doesn't God just make all of this go away? Why doesn't God just let me win the lottery or the million-dollar slot machine, because then all of my financial woes would be over?* The sad truth is, if that occurred in either of these scenarios, chances are your true financial problems would only be beginning. What do I mean by that?

I am sure we are all familiar with the stories of some lottery winners: One day they are the working poor, and the next they are fabulously wealthy. What you never hear is that on average, within seven years, they are again the working poor. How is that possible? All you need to do is study scripture like Proverbs 13:11 states, "a sudden fortune dwindles away ..." It takes certain skills and responsibility to handle wealth. These skills and responsibility are honed and developed during the journey of creating wealth. If you possessed such skills necessary for handling wealth, then you would already be wealthy. Does this mean that if you do not possess such skills, you will never be wealthy? Of course not, but chances are very high that you will not remain wealthy for very long without them. If you do not possess them, you can learn them, starting now. You must simply decide to change your mind and heart.

Do you believe that God wants you to be wealthy? This can be a very difficult question if you are struggling financially. I believe that God is a God of goodness, of blessing, and of prosperity. I also believe that God knows what is best for you, and if that entails being wealthy, then you will become wealthy. If you believe you deserve to be wealthy and aren't, then you need to examine your actions, habits, and beliefs. You need to develop your spiritual self, to grow your stewardship skills and discipline needed to handle wealth. This means a great deal of changing and growing is needed before wealth will be granted.

Proverbs 10:24 cautions, "What the wicked man fears overtakes him, what the virtuous desire comes to him as a present." I remember all too well the feeling I had when my money problems were at their worst. I feared not having any money. That is exactly what happened. When I turned my heart around, my finances began to turn around. Blessings began to come to me. Often I was amazed at the blessings I began to experience. I came to realize everything that was happening, was happening for a reason.

You are in the exact place you have chosen to be financially. If you are in debt, it is because you have chosen to be in debt. Maybe you are thinking, "I did not choose to have my car engine go out. I did not choose to have my furnace fail. I didn't choose to get sick." No, you didn't choose these things, but you did choose how you would handle them, and you did choose to not be prepared for when they occurred. Most importantly, you are choosing your spiritual reaction to financial adversity and success.

Does adversity increase or decrease your faith? Adversity should increase your faith. If it decreases your faith, you have identified your problem. What do I mean by that? I want you to think for a moment. Is pride the sin here? If your faith decreases when you have adversity, are you placing pride between yourself and your reliance on God? Proverbs 11:2 states, "Pride comes first, disgrace comes after; with the humble wisdom is found."

When I let that proverb sink into my heart, I found myself realizing I was suffering from pride. When I began to humble myself to God and what was occurring in my life, my situation changed. I began to understand things I did not understand earlier.

Let's look at an opposite situation. How do you act when you have a surplus of money? Does life become less anxious? Do your worries seem to go away for a while? Does your faith increase or decrease, or do you really not think about it? Your faith should increase. If it decreases then you have discovered your problem. Is it wise for you to think God will bless you with abundance and prosperity if it decreases your faith? Again, the sin of pride comes into question. Do you not need God anymore because your money becomes your fortress?

Let's look at the third scenario, that of not thinking about God when you experience abundance. This is a very common occurrence. We often turn to God in times of trouble because we have nowhere else to turn. The wise practice would be to remain reliant on God in good times as well as bad.

Your faith while in poverty or riches is most likely a testing ground. Proverbs 30:7–9 warns:

> Two things I beg of you, do not grudge me them before I die: keep falsehoods and lies from me, give me neither poverty nor riches, grant me only my share of bread to eat, for fear that surrounded by plenty, I should fall away and say, "Yahweh— who is Yahweh?" or else, in destitution, take to stealing and profane the name of my God.

Take a few minutes and reread these last paragraphs. Think about your faith during times of scarcity and abundance. Does it increase or decrease? Understand: everything God is putting into your life has a purpose. Pray for wisdom and understanding so as to grasp his purpose. God loves you deeply!

I believe God aches when his children are hurting financially. As a parent, how do you feel when you see your child(ren) suffer or struggle? You want to jump right in and save them. I think good parents will allow their children to feel some pain, to struggle, and to learn from mistakes. Otherwise, they will grow up weak and untested. This is not to say that you let them deeply suffer but let them struggle. God knows how much you can handle. He will never send you more than you can bear.

Did you know that a mother eagle builds her nest out of thorny branches and bushes? It's true! She builds the outer nest of this material to protect her babies from predators, and then she lines it with grass and soft downy feathers on the inside. When the baby eaglets are hatched they are born into a soft, cozy and warm nest. As they age, the mother eagle begins to remove the downy feathers and grass from the nest. The nest becomes increasingly uncomfortable for the eaglets. The thorny branches begin to poke and stick the babies. The babies soon learn to fly and leave the nest. You see, if the mom never did this, the babies would never want to leave the nest.

Eagles weren't born to live in nests; they were born to soar. God intends the same for us. He wants us to soar and become the people we can become. We all have to struggle; we all have to endure discomfort at some point in our lives, so embrace it! God wants you to choose; he wants you to choose him! Your financial situation is no different.

Anything you spend your money on is a choice. We all need a place to live and food to eat and some sort of transportation and some type of utilities to provide heat, light, and water. The choices we all have are where we live and how much we pay, what food and how much, whether we can truly afford the new car or any car at all. We do have some decisions as to how much of the utilities we use. You can keep the thermostat lower, the AC off, and the lights off when not in use so as to minimize utility expenses. Any spending outside these areas is discretionary. That means you have *complete* control over when and how much of this type of spending you do in any given month.

Remember the verse from Haggai? Haggai 1:5–8, the part about the wage earner putting his wages into a purse that is riddled with holes? What this says to me is that God will often *not* bless someone with more if they are incapable of handling what they now have. What sense does it make to bless you with more money if you are doing a poor job handling what you now have? If God did choose to bless you with more, chances are very good you would just have bigger debt problems than you do. The problem does not stem from lack of money, but rather how the management of that money has occurred.

This last statement is a profound universal truth, the law of "sowing and reaping." You *must* learn to handle properly what you have now, before you can expect and receive the blessings of increase.

It is counterproductive to "wish" or expect to "win" or "gamble" your way out of debt. A healthy and righteous attitude would be to know that you did not create the problem overnight and it certainly will not be solved overnight. Accepting where you are and how you got there will go a very long way toward fixing your problem. It is very important to remember successes in personal finances are 20 percent know-how and 80 percent attitude. Having a proper attitude about debt and becoming debt-free are the keys to financial success.

What attitude should you have about debt? You should despise it with every fiber of your being! If I were to tell you debt is a form of slavery, would you eagerly seek entering into it? Proverbs 11:29 states, "He who misgoverns his house inherits the wind, and the fool becomes the slave to the wise."

Let's examine the last passage. Have you ever tried to own the wind? If you could, you might become quite wealthy, but as you know the wind can be very elusive. One minute it's there; the next it's gone. The thought of misgoverning one's house is not a pleasant thought. We know what happens to rulers and politicians who misgovern. They are often relegated to the trash heap of history. It is foolish to go into debt to purchase unnecessary things, and yet some people fall prey to the temptation of instant gratification. Why such foolishness? The reasons are quite simple; it is because we are self-centered, greedy, proud, jealous, and envious. The solution is just as simple. Don't go into debt by purchasing a home or an automobile that you cannot afford or anything else that is beyond your means.

Ecclesiasticus (Sirach) 18:30–33 says:

> Do not follow your lusts, restrain your desires. If you allow yourself to satisfy your desires, this will make you the laughingstock of your enemies. Do not indulge in luxurious living, nor get involved in such society. Do not beggar yourself by banqueting on credit when there is nothing in your pocket.

The Bible is very clear about debt with this passage. You should not be banqueting on credit when there is nothing in your pocket to pay for it. A very good rule of thumb would be: do *not* spend money you do not have, *ever!*

If everyone operated along this line of thinking, how many people would be having financial difficulties? One thing is for sure: far, far fewer people than are having financial problems today.

It is foolish to purchase things on credit that depreciate rapidly or never had real long-standing value to begin with. Examples here might include new automobiles, vacations, food, or clothes, to mention just a few. Again, Ecclesiasticus (Sirach) 20:12 reads, "There is a man who buys much for little, yet pays for it seven times over."

The most astounding part of this passage, apart

from its simplicity, is that it was written approximately 2,100 years ago. It is amazing what has changed in the last fifty years; it is ironic that the wisdom of the ages remains unchanged.

Over the last several years, I have noticed a dramatic increase of commercials on radio and television talking about erasing debt.

Not too long ago I was en route to teach a class on the eight steps. The drive was during rush hour and would normally take fifteen minutes to complete. That day it took half an hour. While listening to the radio during this brief commute, I heard no less than seven commercials on debt services.

I was amazed. I could not believe what I was hearing. Most all of the commercials stated something along the lines of, "If you have more than $10,000 of credit card debt you need to call us. We can completely fix your problem. We will share with you secrets that the banks and credit cards companies don't want you to know. This isn't debt consolidation or bankruptcy. We will cut your debt in half. You will *never* have to pay back any of the money we don't settle. You deserve a life again. We will do all the work for you." They even had people providing testimonials: "I did this program and saved myself over $20,000 in credit card debt. I have my life back and can live again. They did all the work for me!"

Are you familiar with the commercials that are being referred to? If you listen to the radio at all, you know exactly the commercials I am speaking of. When such commercials are broadcast, I want

to scream. I want to be very clear when I say this: "These types of debt reduction programs are sinful!"

If you are in a program like this, get out! If you are considering a program like this, don't do it! If you know someone who is considering this type of program, convince them not to. You may be thinking to yourself, *Sinful? Whoa! Wait a minute.*

Let me explain. The whole concept of spending money you do not have and have not yet earned is really crazy, but what is even worse is doing it and then intentionally not paying it back. This is a form of theft! This is in violation of the seventh commandment! "Thou shall not steal." You might be thinking, *Theft?*

Yes, theft! If you have purchased something on credit or bought something without yet having paid for it but made some promise to pay but don't, that is theft, pure and simple! Unless you can return all of the property you have purchased on credit and have not paid for, you have committed theft. There are some things that cannot be returned, such as a vacation or eating at restaurants.

There is no worse way to cripple any future financial success than by committing theft. Proverbs 15:27 states, "He who seeks dishonest gain brings trouble on his house, he who hates bribes shall have life."

What this proverb is saying is that if you seek out dishonest gain (seek to avoid paying back a legitimate debt) by petitioning the creditor to dismiss or drastically cut the amount owed, claiming inability to pay, and not returning the property, you are par-

ticipating in dishonest gain (a form of theft). You are in effect bribing the debt settlement company by paying them to do this on your behalf.

Seeking counsel is a Christian way of handling financial difficulties. However, employing someone like a debt negotiator to fix your financial mess is wrong. It is wrong for two reasons. First, debt negotiation is not Christian because it involves a form of theft, which we have already touched upon. Second, you will have learned nothing about solving the "true" problem of indebtedness, which is your attitude toward debt.

Could you ever imagine Jesus going to the cross and then saying, "Simon, dying for people's sins is scary and difficult. Would you mind doing it for me?" Of course not!

Understanding your financial problem(s) can be scary. You may feel helpless; you may feel embarrassed or humiliated. Proverbs 28:13, speaks of concealing your faults (you will not prosper). The best way to learn is to "DIY" (do it yourself). This does not mean you can't seek advice or have assistance, but if you created the problem, you will be the best to fix it and learn from it. Keep in mind, learning about money is important; you need to live with money the rest of your life. The sooner you learn from your mistakes, the better you will be.

Habakkuk 2:7 warns, "Trouble is coming to the man who amasses goods that are not his, (for how long?) and loads himself with pledges. Will not his creditors suddenly rise, will not your duns awake? Then you will be their victim."

This passage speaks about going into debt by pledging yourself to many creditors. At some point, they do rise up and begin devouring you financially.

I often felt like I was the victim when I received the harassing calls and mail. What I could not deny was that I had purchased things with credit, and when it came time to pay, I didn't. I had to come to the realization that if I wanted to change my financial future, I had to change my attitude about debt. I then had to be ethical and figure out a way to pay back *everyone* to whom I owed money. It did not matter how much. I decided I would pay it back.

Ecclesiasticus (Sirach) 19:1 cautions, "Behave like that and you will never grow rich; he who despises trifles (ignores small details) will sink down little by little."

I could definitely see that happening in my life. It reminded me of the movie *Titanic;* the *Titanic* was my financial situation. I hit the iceberg (health problems), the ship began taking on water (debt and bills), the ship filled, and began to founder; then suddenly, with enough pressure and weight, it rose up out of the ocean and broke in half and sank (we became homeless). Reading passages like those cited above was powerful. There was very little that I could not relate to about debt and its impact upon me and my family.

Being homeless was tough. The physical implications were obvious, but the emotional implica-

tions were much, much greater. My wife blamed me for what had occurred. My wife blamed me for our homelessness. She felt I was trying to force our family to move to Denver. Nothing was further from the truth. We were homeless for a little over a month. I lost my wife's respect and that of the children. They too felt I did it on purpose. The children felt I was trying to make them give up their friends by moving. What can a man do when his family puts him into a position such as this? The respect of my wife and children is the single most important thing to me. I had no room to fail. If I had any chance to preserve my family and my marriage, I would have no choice but to succeed.

We would continue to struggle financially after moving to Denver, but things were stable. My financial plan was working exactly as I had believed it would. However, I did not say, "See, I told you so!" It was more like, "Whew! I'm happy my plan worked." I felt much still needed to be done to make things right with everyone, in order to win back the respect of my family.

It was four years before our lives really began to change. I had decided if I was going to accomplish the goals I dreamed of, my business was not capable of getting me there. I sought the counsel of my oldest brother. The industry he was working in seemed to provide a great living. I discussed with him what he did and other companies he competed against. I began to do a lot of research on the various companies. I decided that I would submit an application to

the biggest company in the industry, which was my brother's main competitor.

I went through four unsuccessful interviews with this company. They kept telling me no. I felt dejected. I could not understand what was needed to prove I was worth taking a chance on. After the fifth interview, they told me they would get back to me in the next couple of days. After three days, I had heard nothing. I began to call them three times a day to inquire about their decision. Every time I called, I was told that the managers were in meetings. After a couple of days of leaving messages and no returned phone calls, I became angry. I decided I would not stop calling until I spoke to a manager and had a decision. I called and spoke to the secretary. I think she intended to place me on hold; I could hear her say, "It's the guy who wants a job. Should I tell him you are in a meeting?" I could hear the manager in the background let out a long exasperated sigh. "Ohhhh! Put him through."

He told me I was the most persistent explicative he had met in a long time. Finally they offered me a position. I sold my business and changed careers. I was now with a Fortune 200 company in sales.

The transition proved to be very difficult. I made my sales quota the very first month, but for the next twelve consecutive months missed big time! I was put on final written notice; they could fire me at any time, for any reason. Matter of fact, the management team that oversaw my work was trying to run me

off by handing me a sales territory that was, by all accounts, unmanageable.

Once again, I found myself against the wall. I had sold my business a year earlier. I was now faced with the prospect of being fired at any moment by a management team that I knew wanted me gone. I had nothing to fall back on. No résumés out to anyone. My wife did not even know that I was at this point. I was afraid to tell her. I don't think I have ever prayed harder in my life than at that time. I was terrified.

My prayers were soon answered. Fortunately for me, most of the management team was transferred to another division. The new team sat down with me, and we had a very direct conversation about my performance.

They felt the slate needed to be wiped clean and that I had not been given a fair chance to succeed. I was about 50 percent of assigned quota at the time. I missed quota the next month, but within a month, everything changed. I began an astounding climb up the sales charts.

I finished the year at 110 percent of quota, and won one of the top sales awards. For the next two years, I did not miss a single month of assigned quota. The year 2001 proved to be my best year ever. I set a number of sales records for the west region. I became the all-time most successful salesperson in our region's history, and won thirteen of the fifteen top sales awards for the year. The two awards I did not win were the two awards I could not qualify for, because I was no longer a rookie. My income, at that time, had more than tripled.

To what did I owe all of this success? Quite simply, I owed everything to God. He had prepared me for what I would encounter. I prayed and studied the Scriptures every day. I focused my life on God and followed the eight steps.

Did that mean I would never struggle or have any financial challenges? Of course not! What God promises his children is that if they trust in him, he will provide everything they need, and more (Matthew 6:25–34).

Climbing Out of Debt

Let's take a moment to revisit the first three steps: Step #1. You *must* have a written budget! This is the road map to free yourself of debt. You *must* know what the facts are. You *must* know how much is coming in and going out. Step #2. You *must* tithe! This is returning to God what is rightfully his. Are you a trustworthy steward? Step #3. Pay yourself first. You *must* create an emergency fund.

Now, with the remaining money, you will create a plan to pay *all* of your creditors. You will create a list of *every* bill or person that you owe. You will then organize the debts from the smallest amount to the largest amount. Do not concern yourself with interest rates at this point, unless two debts are very near equal in amount, then and only then, would you list the debt out of order. For example you owe Master-Card $1,500, with an interest rate of 21 percent, and you owe Macy's department store $1,450, it has an interest rate of 10 percent. In this case, it would make

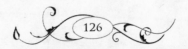

sense to list MasterCard first because of its higher interest rate.

After listing your debts, you will provide a copy of your budget and debt plan to everyone you owe money. It is wise to keep in mind Proverbs 28:13, which reads, "He who conceals his faults will not prosper, he who confesses and renounces them will find mercy."

This says, by admitting your faults to your creditors, you shall find mercy; if not by them, than at least, by God. Most all creditors will appreciate your effort. You are demonstrating to them that you are taking responsibility for the debts and that you have a plan to meet your responsibilities.

Next, you will send a rightful portion of money to each creditor every month, on time. This portion, at first, may not seem to them a fair amount, but once they understand your plan, they most often will not complain. You must contact your creditors if your situation changes, for good or bad. If your situation improves, you should send them, rightfully, an increased amount.

Let me go into detail as to exactly how this works. Let's say you have $900 of discretionary income after tithing, paying yourself first (an emergency fund), and expenses ("the big five"—housing, food, utilities, transportation, and clothing).

I want to clarify what discretionary income is. Most people think of it as the money left over after "all bills and expenses" have been paid. I want you to think about this differently. I want you to view dis-

cretionary as *any* expenditure outside "the big five." If you think about it, discretionary means "to choose." You *choose* to have a credit card, you *choose* to have a gas card, and you *choose* to have a car payment.

In this example, Ford Credit is listed as a debt. This type of "expense" is often listed in "the big five" under transportation as well. I want to be clear: it is debt! We are going to discuss it in this context.

You have the following debts: Ford Credit, $9,300 with an 8 percent interest rate, MasterCard $2,100 with an 18.9 percent interest rate, Visa $4,400 with a 22.9 percent interest rate, Chase Bank loan $3,190 with an interest rate of 8 percent, Texaco $825 with a 16 percent interest rate, Macy's $680 with an interest rate of 18 percent, and medical bills of $700, $400, $540, $75. You will arrange your debt sheet to look like this:

Debt:	Amount Owed	Current Payment
Medical Bill	$75	$10
Medical Bill	$400	$20
Medical Bill	$540	$20
Macy's	$680	$45
Medical Bill	$700	$20
Texaco	$825	$45
MasterCard	$2,100	$110
Chase Bank Loan	$3,190	$145

Visa	$4,400	$125
Ford Credit	$9,300	$325
Totals	$22,210	$865

Your current payments total $865. You have $900 of discretionary income. This leaves you $35 of income to pay off your debt. Continue to send your current payment to all of your creditors, with the exception of the smallest debt. You will apply all of the remaining income to this debt ($900 - $865 = $35). Your new payment for the smallest debt will be your $10 (current payment) + $35 (remaining money) for a total of $45. You will have this debt cleared up in less than two months.

After the smallest debt has been paid off (the $75 medical bill) you will then apply all remaining money to the next smallest debt (the $400 medical debt). You will continue to send in the same current payments on all other debts. Your second debt (again a medical debt) has a minimum payment of $20 (current payment), add to it the $35 (remaining money) plus $10 (the old medical debt payment amount) for a total of $65 (total new payment). You will have this second debt paid off in five and a half months. You will continue this process until *all* of your debts have been paid. This process, in this example, will take about two years to complete.

Most people are amazed when I demonstrate this process. Before they began, they had no reasonable hope that they could pay off these debts. Showing

them the mathematical progression of this method is powerful.

For you to be successful in eliminating your debt, you *must* be committed to not incurring new debt for any reason! This is why it is imperative to have an emergency fund.

If I told you (and this were your scenario) that you could be absolutely free of over $22,000 of debt and have over $12,000 of cash saved in three years, would you believe me? Most people, perhaps even yourself, find this difficult to believe when they are drowning in debt. Believe me, it is possible. Keep reading, because in step #5 all will be made clear.

I have been asked, "Is all debt bad?" I have to reply, "Measuring by the standards of scripture, *yes!* If the Bible said debt was okay, then it would be. No one said following God's standards were easy."

The follow-up question is more challenging: "How do you expect to buy a house then?"

This is a fair question. What I think needs to be considered is this: What would your life look like if you had never had debt, if you never had an ongoing car payment(s), ongoing credit card payment(s), loan payment(s), etc.? And if you had the same income? Would you not be able to save a tremendous amount of money quickly, even enough to buy a house using cash?

If you taught your children these principles and were able to pass on significant amounts of wealth to them, would they not then be able to buy their homes with cash? The point is, our lives would be very different if no one had any debt. The banks, finance, mortgage, and any other money-lending institutions would probably disagree, but I think it might be wise to consider this very different way of life.

Many financial counselors claim it is wise and financially prudent to use at least one, if not several credit cards to maintain a high "FICO" (Fair Isaac Corporation) credit score. They even go to great lengths to educate people on all the ins-and-outs of different credit card company rules, how to read and audit the credit card statement, reading the fine print in the contracts, account balance transfers, and how to become an "expert" credit card user. The only reason you need a "FICO" score is if you want to continue participating in the rat-race of debt!

Let's use the following analogy when obtaining or continuing to handle credit cards. Play along with me: Let's say a snake salesman talks you into obtaining a number of baby snakes. He educates you on exactly how to handle them, feed them, and care for them. He demonstrates to you that through "professional handling" of the snakes, you will never have to worry about ever being bitten. You watch him handle the snakes, and he seems to do well. They look kind of cute and relatively harmless. After all, they are babies, and what harm can they be? You fall for his charm and take them home to make them pets. *Are you out of your ever-loving mind?* These are snakes! They are dangerous even when handled professionally. All snake handlers have been bitten at

some point. That is what snakes do! I want you to view credit cards as snakes. Get my point?

Is it not wiser to *avoid* the potential entrapment of using credit cards than *resisting* the temptation of overspending by using them? Do you understand that credit card companies can change "the rules" whenever they want? They can change your interest rate from 9 percent to 21 percent or higher. They will almost certainly change your interest rate if you make a payment that is late. It is only a matter of time before one of these snakes bites you!

Does God's way mean we should not be using credit cards? Well, Proverbs 16:8 says, "Better to have little and with it virtue, than great revenues and no right to them." This passage clearly states that it is better to have few possessions that you own and the virtue that comes from having paid for them in full, then to own possessions that are not yours, because you have yet to pay for them. It might be prudent to remember that credit cards have the habit of fattening your wallet just before they thin it! [18]

Many people find out too late what credit's (debt's) potential is to enslave and destroy your financial future. I find it amusing that the biggest advocates for credit are people trying to sell you something or people wanting to lend you money. Debt is a very profitable business (for the lender).

Can someone function in this society without the use of credit cards? I'm a living example that you can live in the world today without a credit card. I had several at one time, but I have not owned a credit card since 1989. After accumulating several thousands of dollars of debt on them, I could no longer afford the payments. I closed the accounts in 1989 and cut them up. It took years to pay them off. This was before I had discovered "the eight steps."

One of the goals I set when we were homeless was that we would not buy a home until we were debt free. We purchased our first and only home without having revolving credit. My credit report was many pages long and most of it was negative information. It showed many debts and all of the problems I had dealing with those. But every debt on it was listed as having been paid. Buying a home for me was much easier because I had a pile of cash and no debt. I discuss buying a home in step #7 without having "revolving credit-card history." One of my daughters and her husband bought their first home following this same advice. Neither of them has ever owned a credit card.

What Your Children Need to Know about Debt

The way you conduct your life and how you handle and view debt will most often be repeated by your children. The Bible teaches us that there is no good debt, except the debt of mutual love. Children need to learn to despise debt. They should fear it. They should be taught that debt is a form of slavery and should be avoided at all costs. Teach them not to spend money that they have not yet earned. Teach them that they will always have more desires than money. They must learn to live with this fact.

You must teach your children that credit cards are not money. By using them, you are exchanging convenience for freedom. There is nothing a credit card can do for you that a pile of cash cannot, except charge you interest for the convenience of having them. You must teach your children that even though society teaches that you *must* have a credit card, it is

wiser not to. They are unnecessary! You must teach your children to avoid falling into the trap of debt by overspending. You must teach them there is no virtue in trying to impress people with possessions and that trying to compete with others on possessions is wrong!

Children have the natural tendency to desire things immediately. They must learn both patience and preparation. Patience will provide the ability for them to properly consider the ramifications of their decision(s). Preparation will provide the ability for them to properly plan for needed or wanted expenditures. Patience and preparation will develop a proper attitude. A proper attitude toward debt will strengthen their character enabling them to resist engaging in foolish and impulsive spending. Possessing this proper attitude will shape and mold them into a skillful steward. Your result will be the result that God expects of you as a parent.

If your children are older and already have debt, demonstrate to them through example, how to rid themselves of it, by following step #4 yourself. It is never too late to discuss with them the virtue of becoming and remaining debt-free. To learn this virtue they must learn how to handle the impulse and desire to overspend.

Eliminate Debt—In Review

The Bible does not speak well of financial debt. If you have financial debt, it is wise to eliminate it as soon as possible. An effort should be made to pay all legitimate debts in full. Your life will be more orderly and blessed. Eliminate debt (everything up to the house mortgage) by arranging your smallest balance owed to the largest balance owed regardless of interest rate. The only time you should take something out of order (balance owed) is when you have two debts that are nearly equal in balance owed; then, and only then, should you be concerned with the interest rates of the debts.

Scriptures to live by:

> Proverbs 11:29 (If you misgovern your house, you will become a slave to the wise.)

Ecclesiasticus (Sirach) 18:30–33 (Do not indulge in living luxuriously, spending money you do not have.)

Ecclesiasticus (Sirach) 20:12 (There are people who buy much with little and pay for it seven times over with interest.)

Habakkuk 2:7 (Trouble will come to the person who amasses things that are not his—not paid for.)

Proverbs 16:8 (It is better to have few things that you own than having many that you do not own.)

STEP #5—A FULLY FUNDED EMERGENCY FUND
(SIX MONTHS OF INCOME)

Constructing A Sound Financial Future (Without Credit Cards)!

I feel this step is really the continuation of step #3 (pay yourself first). I have been asked why separate step #3 and step #5? Why not continue to pay yourself first all along? Remember in step #3 (pay yourself first) you are required to establish a *minimum* emergency fund of at least $1,500. Then you stop funding (paying yourself) until you have completed step #4 (eliminate debt). Then and only then you will proceed to step #5. Also, my understanding of Scripture leads me to believe that God wants us to be balanced. Remember Proverbs 11:1?

The famous passage of Ecclesiastes 3:1–8 speaks of there being a time for everything and everything has a time. I believe this to indicate there is a time to

pay ourselves and a time to refrain from paying ourselves. Again, God wants us to be balanced. If you continued to pay yourself through step #4 (eliminate debt), your journey would last considerably longer. Experiencing success quickly, by paying down debt, is important to shaping your attitude. A person can become discouraged if no measurable progress is made after a period of time.

I often liken the journey of eliminating debt to going to the dentist (no offense to dentists or their trade, I just feel everyone can relate going to the dentist) for much needed work.

Are you the type of person who likes spreading your pain out over a long period of time, or are you the type who wants to go and get it over with as quickly as possible? Let's face it, work needs to be done, and I don't think God will hold it against you either way, although he may sometimes set the timetable for you.

What does it mean to have a fully funded emergency fund? Ideally, a fully funded emergency fund is having at least six months of income saved. This may seem like an amazing amount of money to someone who is financially struggling. How could someone who earns $40,000 per year save $20,000? The answer is quite simple. Once the most powerful wealth-building tool (your income) is freed from most debt, it actually can be quite easy. It may take two to three years, but once it

> *"Do you rely on God or credit cards in your times of need?"*

has been accomplished, you will have an amazingly solid financial foundation to build long-term wealth.

Once debt has been conquered, you will have a fairly large discretionary income from which to begin your quest to accomplish step #5. Do you remember our debt payment example from step #4? That example had $900 of discretionary income. Once the debt (with the exception of the mortgage) was paid, the $900 can then be applied to fully funding your emergency fund. Nine hundred dollars is a lot of money to be saving each month. If you did this for one year, you would have $10,800 plus your $1,500 emergency fund. You now have $12,300 in savings. See, I told you this was what you would have. Now if you did this for twenty-four months, you will have accumulated $21,600! Your emergency fund is completely funded.

It's no mystery that most people's lifestyles are tied closely to their earnings; stated differently, most people spend everything they earn, sometimes a little more, sometimes a *lot* more!

Often people, who are having difficulty financially, do nothing to address their problems. Even when their income increases, they continue to expand their lifestyle, so their problem does not change. In fact it will often get bigger, and more complex.

Mastering the first step, "a written budget," will provide the tool by which you can properly control your standard of living. It is very important that as your financial picture begins to improve, you *do not* increase your spending. In some instances, it is wise

and prudent to step down a rung or two on lifestyle. Keep in mind this action is temporary. During this step, the groundwork will have been laid for never needing to possess credit cards. I have counseled many people through varying degrees of indebtedness, and the two most common reasons people were reluctant to give up their credit cards were (1) "what if..." and (2) "just in case..." What if I have an emergency? I need it just in case!

What this really boils down to is the issue of financial security. People think credit cards are emergency funds. They think credit cards are security blankets. Credit cards are horrible security blankets! When used for these purposes, you are exchanging security for freedom.

Now is the time to reflect about your situation with credit cards. I would like for you to take a moment to write down the following questions and your answers on a separate sheet of paper. The questions are: Why do you possess credit cards? Why do you feel you need to posses credit cards? Could you live or do you want to live without them? How are your credit cards affecting your faith in God? Are you relying upon God or credit cards to provide for you in moments of need? What would it take for you to give them up?

Taking the time to honestly answer the aforementioned questions will shed light on where your attitude toward credit is. Remember, successes in personal finances are 20 percent know-how, and 80 percent attitude. Dependence on credit cards is an attitude issue.

Maybe you think you don't have a credit card problem at all. Even if you feel you handle credit cards wisely, by paying them in full each and every month, can you be a better steward by not using them? Many studies have shown that purchases made on credit cards tend to be impulse purchases, more so, than if you paid cash. Statistics show credit card users buy 18 percent more goods and services than they would have had they paid cash. This 18 percent more in discretionary spending is due entirely to impulse purchasing. There is a psychological aspect involved in cash transactions that does not occur when using a credit card. Think about this. I firmly believe it is more painful to pay in cash then to use credit cards. When you pay with cash, your mind will connect with what it took to earn that money. People become more choosey as to how the spend their hard-earned money. Therefore, less impulse buying is likely to occur.

Here is an example: Let's say you have $35 in your wallet or purse and you are food shopping. You have your list: milk, bread, meat, eggs, cereal, pizza, donuts, beer, soda, chips, ice cream, fruit, vegetables, and canned goods. You mentally add everything up and it comes to about $50. You realize, *Wow! I don't have enough. Do I put the other stuff back? No, I will just use my credit card.* Now you spent $50 instead of the $35 you thought you would. I proved my point. Do you really need all of the other things that put

you over the $35 you originally intended to spend (the pizza, beer, chips, ice cream, and donuts)?

Now that you have had a chance to reflect what your attitude toward credit is, what are you going to do about it? Will you commit to changing your attitude?

If you are a credit card user, Proverbs 22:7 states, "The rich man lords it over the poor, the borrower is the lender's slave." Ponder for a moment the last passage. The rich (the banks, the credit card and finance companies) purchase your freedom, often at a rate of 12, 15, 18, or even 22 percent, or sometimes higher. Is it wise stewardship to operate in this manner?

With simple planning and a little discipline, there should be no reason to ever need a credit card. What can a credit card do better than $20,000 of cash, except charge you high interest?

My point is, do not turn to credit cards for security, emergencies, or convenience. Proverbs 24:30–34 strongly cautions:

> By the idler's field I was passing, by the vineyard of a man who had no sense, there it all lay, deep in thorns, entirely overgrown with nettles, its stone wall broken down. And as I gazed I pondered I drew this lesson from the sight, A little sleep, a little drowsiness, a little folding of the arms to take life more easily, and like a vagrant, poverty is at your elbow and, like a beggar want.

Sure it is easy to rely on credit cards for emergencies and security, but just like the idler, you will know poverty and want. Understand that your

financial security needs to be tended to, just like the vineyard.

Debts are the nettles that overgrow your financial vineyard. Just like a gardener, you must properly tend to your financial garden. This requires diligence, persistence, and discipline. Credit cards can appear to be an easy way to manage your finances, but just like a thicket of thorns, you have a very good chance of eventually getting tangled and stuck.

Living a Christian life is not easy for many reasons. We are called to carry ourselves differently than someone who does not know Christ. We are called to enter through the narrow door (Luke 13:22 "The narrow door").

Jesus said we should enter through this narrow door because many will try through the broad door and not succeed. This teaching clearly set the expectation that Christ's followers are to act different from all others. How does this apply to finances? By using credit, you are like everyone else who is trying to gain access through the broad door. Society is obsessed with credit and credit scores. Do not fall prey to this way of thinking. Taking the narrow door (applying the financial steps that the Bible has laid out) will provide security and freedom that most people could never imagine. Faithfully following step #5 (fully funded emergency fund) is following the narrow road, because few will have the discipline to follow it to its conclusion. Those who are wise will know financial peace and success.

Why is it important to have saved such a large

amount of money? The answer is that there are many things that occur in life that if you did not have such reserves your financial house could be jeopardized. The reason for such reserves might include things that involve health, income, employment, or even natural disasters.

The fact is one could probably never think of all the reasons needed for this amount of money, but wouldn't it be nice if, when the need came, you had it?

I have counseled families where the husband or wife or both have lost their job(s), or someone in the household became sick or disabled. This could even have been a child. When this happens, it can become necessary that one of the parents is required to care for the child full time.

If your family is in a position of needing two incomes and can now only produce one, having six months of money in reserve can save the family. These reserve funds can buy you precious time and provide options. Again, remember the ant and grow wise!

Everyone remembers Hurricane Katrina. Many of the people affected by Katrina were very poor. They remained in New Orleans because they had nowhere else to go. They did not have the resources to evacuate.

Imagine if most everyone who was affected by that immense natural disaster had been practicing the eight steps. If they had had six months of income saved, most of their situations would have been dramatically different. A sound financial foundation prepares you for the unknown. It is very important that you understand you do not have to make a large sum of money to have and maintain a solid financial house.

I have counseled a number of single moms on welfare or retired folks on fixed incomes. The results were the same. Financial independence is difficult to achieve on low or fixed income, but one can acquire financial dignity. You can improve your life and have stability when life throws you a curve ball. Having six months or more of income saved can put you there.

What Your Children Should Know about Saving for Emergencies

What, if anything, are you teaching your children about saving for financial emergencies? You should be teaching them that it will never be a question of *if* a financial emergency will happen, but *when!* Financial emergencies (winters) are a part of life. The question becomes, "Will your children, because you have taught them, be prepared to handle the financial emergency?" The wisdom in preparing for such an emergency will contribute to their long-term financial success. You must teach your children that there is a great deal more satisfaction in *saving* money then there is in *spending* money!

Your children should learn the value that discipline brings to hard work. Hard work will provide the ability to earn sufficient income from which future wealth is created. Discipline provides for the development of healthy financial habits. The healthy habit of "paying themselves a portion of everything they earn" will develop their character. Such character is needed to handle wealth!

A Fully Funded Emergency Fund—In Review

Paying yourself first—establishing a "full" emergency fund (six months of income in savings)—is critical for long-term financial security. Reflect on how you feel about your credit cards. Are you using them as a financial safety net? What would it take to rid yourself of those credit cards? You *must* protect yourself from the consequences of unemployment, illness and disability, and natural disasters. It can mean the very survival of your family. If achieving financial stability, dignity, or independence, is your goal, having at least six months of income in savings (in cash), is a must!

Scriptures to live by:

Proverbs 22:7 (The poor man, the borrower, is the rich man's slave.)

Proverbs 24:30–34 (By not being disciplined, poverty will come upon you; you will find your financial garden overrun with thorns.)

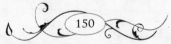

STEP #6—FULLY IMPLEMENT RETIREMENT SAVINGS

Discovering this step was a surprise. I had discovered budgeting, confirmed tithing, learned about paying myself first, and eliminating debt. I had always thought saving for retirement was common-sense important but had no idea the Bible prudently required it the way it did. Most people have great difficulty thinking about retirement because it is often so far into the future. That is one reason, I believe, why saving for retirement is not properly done.

I learned about investing when I was in high school from my mom and oldest brother. They showed me how a very small amount of money, say $50 per month, could become a very large sum of money, if invested faithfully, for a long period of time. Fifty dollars per month was $600/year for 40 years = $24,000. It was also at this time that I was introduced to the concept of compound interest. A

profound simple truth to remember about compound interest is "People who understand compound interest collect it; people who don't, pay it!"

Compound interest is like magic. As a teenager, I was introduced to "the rule of 72." The "rule of 72" is how compound interest works. It states, "If you divide 72 by your rate of return (say 12%); 72 divided by 12 = 6. Meaning, this is the number of years it will take to double your investment (every six years)." The number 72 is a constant. It will never change. In my case, the $24,000 would become over $489,000 if invested over forty years! Not bad for $50/month at 12 percent!

> *"People who understand compound interest collect it; people who don't, pay it!"*

It might be surprising to learn that this simple concept, "the rule of 72," is not taught in economics classes or colleges of business or finance. Yet it is fundamental in understanding the magic of compound interest. This left a deep impression on me as a sixteen-year-old.

The Magic of How Compound Interest Works

If you invest $50 per month, this is what your investment would look like from ten years to sixty years earning a 3 percent return to 15 percent return. Notice the effect the percent of return has on the impact of your investment. But especially notice the effect that time has on the return. It is most important to start early!

Interest Rates

Years	3%	6%	9%
10	$6,990.00	$8,160.00	$9,550.00
20	$16,380.00	$22,780.00	$32,170.00
30	$29,010.00	$48,960.00	$85,720.00
40	$45,970.00	$95,850.00	$212,480.00
50	$68,770.00	$179,810.00	$512,580.00
60	$99,410.00	$330,180.00	$1,223,010.00

Years	12%	15%
10	$11,200.00	$13,150.00
20	$45,990.00	$66,350.00
30	$154,040.00	$281,590.00
40	$489,650.00	$1,152,330.00
50	$1,531,990.00	$4,674,980.00
60	$4,769,330.00	$18,926,060.00

Let's examine another investment table and see how important it is to start early. In this example we will look at Investors A and B. Investor A starts early and invests $2,000 each year for six years, and then stops investing. (Currently Investor A is twenty years old.) Investor A lets his money grow until he reaches age sixty. Investor B is also twenty years old, but waits seven years before beginning to invest. In the seventh year, Investor B invests $2,000 each year and does not stop until he reaches age sixty. Both Investors A and B receive 12 percent interest on their investments. Investor A has invested a total of $12,000, while Investor B invested $70,000. Who has the most money after both Investors A and B turn sixty years of age?

	Investor A		Investor B	
Age	Payment Amount	Balance	Payment Amount	Balance
20	$2,000	$2,240	0	0
21	$2,000	$4,759	0	
22	$2,000	$7,559	0	0
23	$2,000	$10,706	0	0
24	$2,000	$14,230	0	0
25	$2,000	$18,178	0	0
26	0	$20,359	$2,000	$2,240
27	0	$22,803	$2,000	$4,759
28	0	$25,539	$2,000	$7,559
29	0	$28,603	$2,000	$10,706
30	0	$32,036	$2,000	$14,230
31	0	$35,880	$2,000	$18,178
32	0	$40,186	$2,000	$22,559
33	0	$45,008	$2,000	$27,551
34	0	$50,409	$2,000	$33,097
35	0	$56,458	$2,000	$39,309
36	0	$63,233	$2,000	$46,266
37	0	$70,821	$2,000	$54,058
38	0	$79,320	$2,000	$62,785
39	0	$88,838	$2,000	$72,559
40	0	$99,499	$2,000	$83,507
41	0	$111,438	$2,000	$95,767

42	0	$124,811	$2,000	$109,499
43	0	$139,788	$2,000	$124,879
44	0	$156,563	$2,000	$142,105
45	0	$175,351	$2,000	$161,379
46	0	$196,393	$2,000	$183,005
47	0	$219,960	$2,000	$207,206
48	0	$246,355	$2,000	$234,310
49	0	$275,917	$2,000	$264,288
50	0	$309,028	$2,000	$298,668
51	0	$346,111	$2,000	$336,748
52	0	$387,644	$2,000	$379,398
53	0	$434,161	$2,000	$427,166
54	0	$486,261	$2,000	$480,665
55	0	$544,612	$2,000	$540,585
56	0	$609,966	$2,000	$607,695
57	0	$683,162	$2,000	$682,859
58	0	$765,141	$2,000	$767,042
59	0	$856,958	$2,000	$861,327
60	0	$959,793	$2,000	$966,926

Notice that Investor B did not catch up to Investor A until age fifty-eight! Remember, Investor A invested $12,000 and Investor B invested $70,000! Who is the better steward?

The Bible frequently addresses the principle of compounding. Various people would receive compounded blessings, often in the form of money and prosperity. An example of this is found in Genesis 26:12–14 when it says, "Isaac sowed his crop in that land, and that year he reaped a hundredfold. Yahweh blessed him and the man became rich; he prospered more and more until he was very rich indeed. He had flocks and herds and many servants. The Philistines began to envy him."

Another passage that demonstrates compounding is to be found in Matthew 13:4–9:

> He said, "Imagine a sower going out to sow. As he sowed, some seeds fell on the edge of the path, and the birds came and ate them up. Others fell on patches of rock where they found little soil and sprang up straight away, because there was no depth of earth; but as soon as the sun came up they were scorched and, not having any roots, they withered away. Others fell among thorns, and the thorns grew up and choked them. Others fell on rich soil and produced their crop, some a hundredfold, some sixty, some thirty. Listen, anyone who has ears!"

How does this parable apply to finances? The seeds are our financial resources. Some falling at the edge and being consumed by birds are good resources but wasted. The seeds falling upon the rock are resources that are simply not applied they way they should be. They do not provide true benefit to the steward. The seeds that were among the thorns are resources that are being choked off by debt. Seeds that fall on fertile ground are resources that are employed properly, according to God's way. They are the resources that will produce "biblical compounding."

Applying this parable to finances is necessary if you desire to become a "true steward." Your responsibility as a financial steward is to seek the "fertile soil" in which to sow and to avoid the "rocks and thorns" that impede God's financial plan for you. One must plant his crop for future harvesting. Without employing resources, there will be no future harvest. Consider Ecclesiasticus (Sirach) 29:11, "Invest your treasure as the Most High orders, and you will find it more profitable than gold."

Compounding is the most powerful financial principle encountered in all of my studies of the scriptures. That is why mastering step #7 "Saving for Retirement" is a must!

How Much Do Poor Financial Decisions Cost? Plenty!

Earlier in the book I made the statement that continuous car payments are costing you more than *$400,000 in future wealth*. I want to drive (no pun intended), the point home by demonstrating just how much those ongoing car payments are really costing! Once you understand the power of compound interest, you will be better equipped to make more prudent stewardship decisions regarding the purchase of your car(s).

Statistically, 81 percent of all new car purchases are financed, while only 56 percent of all used cars purchased are financed, according to a Department of Commerce Consumer Expenditure Survey Anthology from 2003. The average monthly payment for a new car (1999–2000) was $399. The average monthly payment for a used car (1999–2000) was $273, according to that same survey. I feel safe stating that the

price of cars since 1999 has not decreased. I would feel equally safe by stating peoples' habits haven't changed either. Consider the Federal Reserve's Statistical Release for September, 2008, which states the average amount financed on a new car was $26,643, with the average length of financing (maturity of the loan), being 65.4 months. The average length has steadily increased since 2003 from 61.3 months to their current levels.

Most people need some type of transportation; the real question is to buy new or used? Before the question is answered, it must be known that, on average, *most* new cars depreciate (lose value) at a rate of 50 percent over a 3 year period. That means, if you paid $35,000 for your new vehicle, after three years of ownership, its value will be something close to $17,500! Now, if I were your financial advisor and you entrusted with me the same $35,000 to invest on your behalf, and 3 years later, I reported back to you that your $35,000 had become $17,500, are you going to be happy with me? Would you remain my client for very long with those results? Yet most people are not only doing this, they are *paying interest* (finance costs) in addition to the car payment, to have such results! This is financial insanity! Remember Proverbs 17:16 (What good is money in a foolish hand? To purchase wisdom when he has no sense.)? It may be prudent indeed, to remember this advice.

Because most people who buy cars, finance them, and finance them on average for 65 months (5.5 years). They never stop making payments on their vehicles. They buy another vehicle, either before, or soon after, paying off their current vehicle. Now, let's examine the future wealth lost by choosing to have on-going car payments.

Let's say we have person A and person B buying vehicles. Each owns a car worth $12,000. Person A trades in his current car for $12,000 credit toward a new $35,000 car. He decides to finance the balance of $23,000 with a rate of 7 percent for 5 years. Person A will pay $4,325 in interest charges ($23,000 financed at 7 percent for 5 years = $4,325). Person A's payment would be $455.42. Person B delays for 2 years his purchase of a vehicle (a concept called *delayed gratification*—I demonstrate this concept in greater detail in the next chapter). Person B saves what the payment would have been ($455.42) over a 2 year period ($455.42 x 24 months = $10,930.08). Person B then trades in his car, now worth $10,500 (depreciated from $12,000). Person B does not want to finance his car so he buys a 3 year old used car for the $21,400 that he now has available ($10,500 trade-in + $10,930 saved = $21,430). The used car that Person B bought, sold for $42,000 new! Yes, Person B bought a used car, but he saved $5,895 in doing so! Now let's examine the long term impact.

Remember, Person A chose to finance his loan for 5 years while Person B saved money for 2 years, Person B uses the 3 additional years of no car payments, and invests the money saved by engaging in *delayed gratification*. After 3 years, following the principle of *delayed gratification* Person B will have saved $16,395

($455.42 x 36 months = $16,395). The total financial impact of this transaction is $22,290 in favor of person B ($5,895 saved purchasing used car + $16,395 saved because he had no car payment = $22,290). Person B invests this money and receives an 8% return on his one-time investment. After 36 years Person B will have accumulated $396,955 ($22,290 compounded at 8% for 36 years = $396,955)! Imagine if this was done multiple times during your lifetime!

My final thought on automobiles is this: let someone else take the hit on the depreciation of a new car and purchase a used car that is at least 3 years old, but still in "like-new" shape. This will make you a more prudent steward, because your actions today will affect your future.

A Vision for the Future

Most people would agree that saving for retirement is important. Some may even say that it is fundamental. If this were true, why then, is it that a vast majority of Americans retire broke (at or below the poverty line)? According to the Economic Policy Institute, 73 percent of retirement income is provided by Social Security, 17 percent by company pensions, and 10 percent from personal savings and investing. The average Social Security payment in 2004 was $954.90 (Social Security Administration). Why is it that a majority of people do not start saving for retirement until after age thirty-five? Americans are living much longer, on average, than their grandparents. Often more money is needed to provide for longer retirements. Many retirees are worrying about outliving their money. It is a sad fact that most Americans do not properly prepare for their "golden years" by prudently saving a consistent amount of money for

a long period of time (thirty-five to forty-five years instead of the twenty to twenty-five that most do). If they properly saved, this vast majority would not be a vast majority, it would be a small minority.

The answer to the problem of inadequate savings is quite simple. People do not save because they do not have a vision, and they do not have the discipline. Proverbs 10:17 says, "The path to life is to abide by discipline, and he who ignores correction goes astray." Remember Proverbs 13:18? It warns, "For the man who rejects discipline: poverty and disgrace; for the man who accepts correction: honor." Both these proverbs strongly encourage discipline and learning from others who have made mistakes or are wiser than yourself. A third proverb that speaks to this very important tenet to wealth building is Proverbs 23:12, which states, "Apply your heart to discipline, and your ears to words that are wise." The lesson here is that we often spend our money on frivolous things every day of the week. What we don't realize is that we are trading our future financial freedom for so many things that, in the grand scheme of life, are worthless!

The most powerful scriptures to be found on the subject, is Ecclesiastes 5:12–16, which says:

There is a great injustice that I observe under the sun: riches stored and turning to loss for their owner. One unlucky venture, and those riches are lost; a son is born to him, and he has nothing to leave him. Naked from his mother's womb he came, as naked as he came he will depart again;

nothing to take with him after all his efforts. This is a grievous wrong, that as he came, so must he go; what profit can he show after toiling to earn the wind, as he spends the rest of his days in darkness, grief, worry, sickness and resentment?

A small amount of discipline can go a very long way when dealing with saving for retirement. The earlier a person can be taught to save a small portion of everything he makes, the better off he will be. Designing your lifestyle to embrace discipline will bring many blessings.

Most teenagers and young adults would rather have a good time, wear nice clothes, drive souped-up cars, and have stereos and cell phones and iPods than save for retirement. Adults on the other hand would rather drive nicer cars, live in nicer homes or apartments, wear nicer clothes, take nicer trips, and eat out more, etc, than save for retirement. The truth is, I could probably write for quite some time on what people would "rather" do with their money than save for retirement. Because people choose to live in this manner, they will most likely never experience the full blessings promised by God. Proverbs 16:20 promises, "He who listens closely to the word shall find happiness; he who trusts in Yahweh is blessed." It is in this simple wisdom that success and happiness reside. Obeying God's words in all their facets and consistently demonstrating discipline are cornerstones to building wealth.

As a boy, I sometimes thought what it would be like to be old. What would I do? What would my life

look like? The only good way to envision my future was to view an older generation like my grandparents. I loved going to visit my grandparents in Kansas. They were always so interesting to me. Their lives were very different from my parents. My mom's dad worked as an electrician for a small town in Kansas, while her mom was mostly a stay-at-home mom. My dad's dad worked in a foundry in the same small town. I never knew my dad's mother because she died when I was very young. My dad's parents were poor and not well educated.

I knew my mom's parents much better. My mom's parents had raised two girls. My parents were raising six boys. My mom's parents' house was a small bungalow and had one bathroom and two bedrooms. When we visited, we slept in the basement and slept on cots or stayed outside in a small tent camper.

All of my grandparents' lives were tempered by the Great Depression. Frugality and resourcefulness were necessities. They never owned credit cards. They paid cash for everything. If they did not have the cash, they did not buy it. My mother's parents saved for a number of years for the down payment to buy their first and only home. The cost of their home was $7,000 in 1949. To earn extra money my grandfather loaded and unloaded a ton of coal for $.50. Having this $7,000 debt over their heads frightened them. They paid it off in seven years. I compare this to today where the average home sells for $225,000.

I feel the lessons to be learned from the Great Depression era have use in today's modern world.

There is wisdom in not incurring a bunch of debt and in practicing delayed gratification (not spending money unless you have it saved). I reflected on these bits of wisdom and began to gain a sense of what I needed to do for my situation. This gave me direction. I knew I needed to sit down and implement a plan.

After two weeks of being homeless, I sat down and wrote out the fifteen things I would most like to accomplish. One was as simple as having $500 in a savings account. Another, much more daunting, was retiring at the age of fifty-two. Here I was, twenty-seven years old, homeless, and broke. My marriage was on the rocks, and I had over $100,000 of debt. I had no idea, at that point, what it would take to achieve the goal of retirement. I believed through my ordeal that I had witnessed some sort of miraculous awakening. I saw clearly what it was that I wanted, and what specifically it would look like.

I often think of Charles Dickens' classic *A Christmas Carol* and its main character, Ebenezer Scrooge, when I think of retirement. You may be saying, "What?"

Ebenezer Scrooge had the benefit of living in the past, present, and future. Through an amazing series of events, he had an epiphany and recognized the error of his ways. He changed after he saw the consequences of his actions and non-actions. If we could see what our actions and non-actions produced in the future, would we continue doing, or not doing, them? Life is too short and precious to sit figuratively on the sidelines and do nothing out of fear or lack of discipline.

Most people operate from the perspective of the past. They allow fear, anxiety, and lack of discipline to control their lives. It is very important to understand that the past is the past. We need to focus on living in the present and have hope and faith for the future. Everything you do, or don't do, will have consequences.

These consequences can range from living a life in monetary desperation to living out your days in comfort and abundance. How do you think the sons and daughters of a king should live?

Most people, for whatever reason, seem to like choosing the former over the latter. The bottom line is that retirement must be a carefully planned event. It requires the ability to envision what the future holds. This is not easily done, but doable. Remember how, as children, we dreamed of doing many things?

When I discuss retirement with people, I often find it necessary to awaken the child in them and get them dreaming again. I need to help people reconnect the head to the heart and soul. Most people, for whatever reason, have stopped dreaming. They have stopped believing that they can accomplish their dreams. It is as if they have taken their hopes, dreams, and desires and shut them off completely and are resigned to living a quiet life of desperation.

The lack of dreams and hope for the future is why so many people play the lottery or religiously watch the TV game shows. Their only hope to have some sense of financial dignity, now and in the future, is to somehow match up the lucky numbers or to appear on a game show and win it all! They are afraid to dream of anything outside of luck.

I have met individuals and married couples who actually said that their strategy for retirement was solely tied to winning the lottery. When asked the obvious question, "What if your numbers are never called?" that's when they looked at each other and did not reply; they knew the answer. They would never be able to retire. They would continue to work, just as their parents did, until they died. They needed to work not because they wanted to, but because they *had* to. If they somehow were able to retire, it required that they had to live on such meager means that they had to dramatically curtail their lifestyle. Is this what God sacrificed his Son for, that his children would live in constant want and need, due to fear?

When counseling people on step #6 (funding retirement), I have asked some tough questions. Questions such as: How do you envision your life when you retire? What kind of income do you want in retirement? Will you be doing what you were meant to do? How would you spend your time? Is there something you dreamed of a long time ago that you wanted to do or accomplish and given up on? Have you discovered your purpose? The "why" are you here? Why is this particular thing so important to you?

I know I have connected with someone after asking these questions when their eyes tear up as they

begin to describe why they want something. They realize how suppressed their dreams had become; they realize how beat up and fearful they have become in regard to accomplishing their dreams.

When someone understands their *"why,"* they have a true sense of purpose. They will go after, and most often succeed, if they know *why* they want to do or accomplish something. When you understand the *why*, you don't care how hard something is or how long it takes or how scared you might be, you simply do it!

God places in our hearts the essence of these dreams. All of us have gifts and uniqueness that, when combined with a purpose, drive us to accomplish amazing feats. A fun exercise to engage in would be: If money were no object, what would you be doing? What would you pursue?

When the lottery is at $1 million it is easy to think in terms of: If I had a $1 million what would I do? Why is it such a leap to believe you could create a million dollars, through disciplined saving? Statistically, your odds are far better that you can earn or create millions by saving a small portion of everything you make, and investing it wisely. The odds dramatically go up from there, if you are doing something you love!

I want you to take a bookmark and place it in this chapter and take a break. I want you to close your eyes and think about what was just asked and said in the previous paragraphs.

You need to answer these questions for yourself.

Are you living the life you believe you were meant to live? If not, then what life do you feel you should be living? What is holding you back from living your ideal life and why? What is your purpose? What are you good at? What type of lifestyle would you like to live and why? What do you want your retirement to look like? What would you do with your time and resources? Why? Following your death, how would you like to be remembered? What would you want said about you and your contributions to your family, your community, and the world?

Once you begin to reconnect the head to the heart, your life will have a new sense of meaning. Often this can be a very overpowering and emotional experience. Embrace it!

Write all your answers in a diary or notepad. As you begin to clarify and solidify your responses, you will gain focus on your dreams. Begin to visualize your answers. What exactly do you want? What exactly does it look like? When this is done correctly, you will feel like you are watching a full-length motion picture, in your mind's eye, titled *Your Life As It Was Meant to Be!* This will be a movie, directed by you, about you, starring you. The most fun part about this is that if you would like to change a scene—no problem—alter the ending—no problem. This movie is whatever you want it to be. Have fun with it!

Basic Balanced Investing—
Biblical Style

Mastering the mental aspects of long-term financial success is critical to successful planning for retirement. I want to now discuss the practical aspects of long-term financial success—the basics. The basics can be very tough when you are dealing with attitudes and habits.

Building long-term wealth requires proper attitudes and habits. Remember the quote, "Successes in finances are 20 percent know-how and 80 percent attitude"? It is critical to ridding your mind of the idea that you must, or will, win the lottery. This is needed to develop the proper attitude that will be required to handle wealth, when you begin your journey. To really drive this point home, you must read and reflect deeply on Proverbs 13:11, "A sudden fortune will dwindle away, he grows rich who accumulates little by little."

What is it about a sudden fortune that makes this proverb true? I am sure we can all recall famous people, or perhaps a lottery-winner story, that illustrates the simple truth about the wisdom of this verse. The truth lies in the fact that to manage immense wealth properly, requires immense character. Until that level of character is achieved, it is often unlikely you will be able to maintain the responsibility that that level of wealth requires.

Does this mean that you could suddenly come into wealth (whether earned, inherited, or won) and not be able to handle it properly? Of course not, but Proverbs 13:11 is meant to be a warning. Stated differently: to whom much is given, much is expected and needed. The exact same can be said of "get-rich-quick" schemes.

Refer to Proverbs 28:20, "A trustworthy man will be overwhelmed with blessings, but he who tries to get rich quickly will not go unpunished."

Another aspect to the wealth-building principles of "management" and "increase" is Proverbs 23:4–5, which cautions, "Do not worry yourself with getting rich, and have nothing to do with dishonest gain. You fix your gaze on this, and it will be there no longer, for it is able to sprout wings like an eagle that flies off to the sky."

A seemingly odd paradox abounds with dishonest gain. I have been asked numerous times, "Why is it that dishonest people seem to always get away with things? They cheat. They steal. They take advantage of others and seem never to be forced to pay a price."

The real question is "If God is a just God, then why does he allow people who act in that manner to flourish?" The answer is not an easy one.

Does the question really reside in envy? Would you like to act in this manner and have no fear of being punished? Take heart, because God promises, in Proverbs 23:17, by stating, "Do not let your heart be envious of sinners but be steady every day in the fear of Yahweh; for there is a morrow, and your hope will not be nullified."

What are we to learn from these proverbs about increasing and investing? Sudden fortunes, get-rich-quick schemes, and dishonest gains play to our emotions of greed, envy, lust, jealousy, and pride. You may recall these are five of the seven deadly sins. We must always keep in mind: Avoid sinning!

The other side of the investing coin is losing money that you have invested. We must guard against blaming others or blaming God. Most often it is our own folly that spoils our fortunes. It is very easy to blame God and others for our financial misfortunes. Proverbs 19:3 speaks to that exact problem. It states, "It is man's folly that spoils his fortunes, yet it is against Yahweh that his heart rages." We must accept responsibility for our own actions and inactions.

The actions you must take are of diligence; you must contribute a portion of your money toward the future. The actions you must not do are to procrastinate; you must not put off saving for retirement. If you are financially unable to invest, you must position yourself to begin investing for retirement as soon as possible. Following "the eight steps" faithfully is critical.

Imagine what your financial future would look like if you had no debt, with the exception of a mortgage. How much money would you be able to save for investing purposes? If we used as our example from previous chapters the $900/month (discretionary income) after-tithing, expenses, and paying yourself first, we want to look at contributing 10 percent of the $4,000 gross income (10% of $4,000/month = $400). The proper amount of funding for retirement is $400/month.

If you have six months of income in savings (from paying yourself first—step #5), as you should, you should also use that money to fund retirement. You should be putting $800/month or $9,600/year into retirement. Where do you invest $9,600/year? There are many investment vehicles from which to choose.

First, if you are employed by a company that offers a 401(k) or a simple IRA, then either of these can be great vehicles in which to invest money, especially if there is company or employer matching funds involved. Let's say you decided to invest your $800/month in a 401(k), and your employer contributes another 3 percent. This is a great deal! If you are putting in $9,600/year and your employer is contributing an additional 3 percent, the employer's contribution is calculated based on your qualified annual earnings of $4,000/month or $48,000/

THOMAS E. ZORDANI

year. The employer's contribution to your retirement fund would be $1,440 each year. This equates to a 15 percent return on your investment. Not bad to start with! This does not include any gains or compounding you may receive from having invested your money in mutual funds or other investment vehicles available in 401(k)s.

Using the "rule of seventy-two" in the above example and receiving a return of say 6 percent (which is very low), your total return would be 21 percent (15 percent on the employer contribution and 6 percent on compounding). Your money would double every 3.4 years. So after three years, you might have something like $70,000; another 3.4 years and you will be at $140,000. As I mentioned before, compound interest is magical!

The whole idea behind investing wisely is keeping it simple and slow. If you have a 401(k) or a simple IRA available at work—use it, especially when employer contributions are involved! If you do not understand what you are doing (in investing your money), find someone who does, and learn from him/her. You do not need to become an expert, but you should learn the basics. You should learn how to calculate the employer contribution. You should learn how to read an account statement, and you should learn something about what funds in which to invest. This can be very intimidating at first, but if you take the time to learn from someone who knows more than you, it will be well worth the effort.

So how do you figure out how much you need to

be saving for retirement? You need to first complete the exercises we discussed earlier in this chapter. You need to know how much money is needed when you retire. Once you know the retirement income number (retirement income to support your desired lifestyle), your needed monthly savings can easily be calculated with a retirement calculator. There are many programs available for free on the Internet. Keep in mind that $48,000 will not buy the same lifestyle thirty years from now. Always take into account inflation. Inflation, over the years, has averaged about 3 percent. Keep in mind "the rule of 72"!

The other aspect of which you want to remind yourself is, do you want or need to save enough to live on the interest of your investments, or do you want to live off a combination of interest and principal? An example would be: You have $1,000,000 saved for retirement. If that $1,000,000 is earning a 5 percent return, that means it is earning you $50,000/ year. If you need $70,000 income (adjusted for inflation), you will begin eating into your $1,000,000 nest egg. Over a period of time, your money will disappear (depending on how long you live). Do you want to outlive your money, or would you like to choose to leave, as an inheritance, to your spouse or other family members any sum of this money? If running out of money scares you, then you will need to adjust your final retirement investment number to encompass living solely off interest. Your nest egg would need something like $1,200,000 to provide a $50,000 annual income adjusted for inflation. This will ensure

that you *never* outlive your money or leave your heirs nothing.

Now that you know how much you need for retirement, you can now figure out how much you need to save, on a monthly basis, to get there. You will know if saving $800/month is going to do for you what you want.

Depending on what your situation is (how old you are, how much you are saving, when you want to retire, and how many years you must save), you will at least have some type of plan to get there. Ninety-six percent of Americans do not have a plan. That is why they retire in poverty or worse, they can never retire.

If your calculations are not working out to your liking, have faith. You can play with the numbers. You can invest more, or you can delay retirement for a few years. You should seek help from a professional. There may be many ways to accomplish your goals. The point is this: you will always miss the goals that are never set.

Balance now needs to be discussed. The matter of balance was discussed earlier (in step #1 and #5 of "the eight steps"). Remember Proverbs 11:1? It told of God loving a just balance. Let's focus on balance for right now and how it would apply to long-term investing and becoming a better steward.

There are three different investment categories, as it pertains to growth, taxing, and drawing upon retirement income. The first category is *tax-now*, the second is *tax-later*, the third and final is *tax-never*.

Tax Now	Tax Later	Tax Never
Mutual Funds	401(k)	Roth IRAs/ Roth 401(k)s
Stocks	403(b)	VUL/Cash Value Life Ins.
Bonds	IRAs/SEP IRAs	
Treasuries	Annuities (Fixed/Variable)	
CDs	Savings Bonds	
Savings Accounts		
Money Markets		

The "tax-now" category is a very common type, perhaps the most common used for investing. This type taxes investments or earnings each and every year they are earned. These would include such investments as mutual funds, stocks, bonds, treasuries, CDs, saving accounts, and money market accounts. These are typically for very current or shorter-term needs and are typically very liquid (easily accessible and quick into cash). Any investment that generates a 1099 (an IRS tax form required for capital gains that are generated from investment income on a yearly basis) at the end of the year will fit into this group.

The problem with the "tax-now" investment vehicle is that its capital growth is slowed due to taxation of that growth. Every year that your investment experiences capital growth (growth of your money), you must report it as income, and you are taxed on that income. Depending on your tax bracket, these taxes can be very high. This type of investment is necessary, because the money is typically very liquid (easily accessible).

The second, "tax-later," is also a very common type used for investing. This vehicle defers the taxation to a time in the future when the retirement income will be drawn upon. The most common types of investments that fit into this category are 401(k)s, 403(b)s, or a number of other qualified plans. Also included in this group would be IRAs and SEPs. Savings bonds and even annuities (both fixed and variable) make up this group.

The concept for IRAs, SEPs, 401(k)s, and 403(b)s is that you, the participant, are able to defer (save) pre-tax money, in investment accounts for the purpose of retirement. Pre-tax means that you do not pay income tax on that money until you withdraw it at retirement. So if you made $4,000/month and were contributing $300/month into a 401(k)-type plan, the government only taxes you on the income left over; in this case, $3,700/month.

These types of investments can be very beneficial

because employers grant some type of contribution, to your retirement account. I highly recommend them if that is the case. The problem with this type of vehicle is that the money is not very liquid. You can withdraw it, but you will pay taxes and a hefty penalty. Most often, the money cannot be withdrawn until age fifty-nine and a half, without penalty. There are some exceptions to this rule, but for the sake of simplicity, I will not discuss it.

The third and final investment category is the "tax-never." This one is rarely used. A lot more people should be using it than they already do because most people do not know about it. There are only a couple of investment vehicles that fit into this category. The first is the Roth IRA and the other is the variable universal life (VUL) or cash-value type life insurance. These investments are funded with after-tax money (take-home pay) so the tax has already been paid. The benefit is that there are no deferred taxes. You will not pay tax on the growth of these investments. These vehicles allow compounding to truly work. The drawback is that the money is not as liquid as the first vehicle— "tax-now." This is definitely for longer-term investing. The money is, however, more liquid than the second investment category— "tax-later"—because of the after-tax status of the money. A drawback for the Roth IRA is that you are limited as to how much you can invest each year ($5,000, if you are single, $10,000, if you are married, and more, if you are over the age of fifty). There are also limits as to who can qualify for a Roth. You will

want to seek guidance from a licensed professional to assess your personal situation.

The variable universal life insurance policy (VUL) and other cash-value life insurance products can be a powerful vehicle for long-term financial savings. These vehicles offer life insurance and investment together. I personally struggled with this concept for a very long time. I firmly believed at the time that life insurance was just that—insurance for your life, not an investment vehicle. I changed my belief about this specific type of investment (the VUL) because I felt that the life insurance companies had changed the investment vehicle to truly benefit the investor. There are many types of insurance products that are horrible for the average person. Specifically, whole-life and universal-life insurance products are very expensive while they generate large commissions for the sales reps. These are not to be considered as a sound type investment for most people. In my opinion, the VUL is a bona fide investment vehicle.

I am sure that I will not be making many friends in the insurance world with my comments, but my purpose is to demonstrate a better way to conduct your finances and not to sell insurance.

The reason I like the VUL is that it allows one to control his investment, and the insurance cost tends to be significantly less than whole-life or universal-life. A large portion of the VUL premium goes into the investment side of the policy. One is able to over-fund the policy as well. This means that, in addition to the premium I pay, I am able to invest up to approximately $13,000 each year into the policy (which depends upon the insurance policy value). This money is fairly liquid, much more so than the Roth IRA. There are no age limits (fifty-nine and a half) to access your money. I found that this particular vehicle is used by many, if not most, very wealthy individuals.

Earlier, I had mentioned balance. What do three different tax categories have to do with balance? Everything! These investment categories are the vehicles needed to be used for retirement. Proper balance requires that each of these vehicles be used. Each has its strengths, and each has its drawbacks. You might ask the question, "If you like the second and third vehicles more than the first, then why put money into the first vehicle?" The answer is the need for balance!

Let's use an example of how this balance demonstrates good stewardship in finances. By putting money into a 401(k)-type account (the second vehicle), you have aggressively funded your retirement plan for many years. Now, suppose you have a balance of $700,000 in your 401(k) for retirement and you would like to have an income of $50,000 annually, at retirement. Remember, the second vehicle is income tax deferred. This means you must pay income tax on *all* of your retirement income that is withdrawn from your 401(k). If you want an annual income of $50,000, you *must* withdraw about $57,000 each year because you must pay income tax on the money. Keep in mind this does not take into account infla-

tion. Twenty years from now $50,000 won't buy the same lifestyle as today. Because of inflation, $67,000 will be needed to maintain the same lifestyle and pay taxes. The $67,000 is more like $75,000 because of the tax liability! The problem of inflation is why the average 401(k)-type account lasts only twelve years rather than the twenty to twenty-five years people may expect or need.

If we look at the same financial situation utilizing a *balanced* approach (investment vehicles), the scenario would look something like this: You have saved $700,000. You invest in a mutual fund (the first-type investment vehicle) and have a balance of $100,000. The 401(k)-type account (the second-type investment vehicle) has a balance of $325,000. You fund a third vehicle (a VUL policy) over a number of years and accumulate a balance of $275,000. Suppose you still want a lifestyle of $50,000/year. We must consider withdrawing money from each of these type investment vehicles so as to make up your $50,000 retirement income. Remember, with the first-type investment vehicle, you do not pay tax on the income, but only on the gains of the previously invested money. The second-type investment vehicle requires that income tax be paid on that (401(k)-type) income. The third investment type vehicle requires no tax on withdrawals, because this account was funded by after-tax money, just as the first investment type vehicle.

Your income stream may look something like this: $4,000 from the first investment-type vehicle,

$23,000 from the second investment-type vehicle, and $23,000 from the third investment-type vehicle. You will be taxed only on the income from the second-type investment vehicle (the 401(k)-type account). Your tax bracket on $23,000 is far lower than a tax bracket of $50,000 income! You will save yourself about $4,000/year in taxes. You are not drawing on any single account too much, allowing your money to work longer and harder for you. The same $700,000 of retirement income will last several years longer due to this practice.

Retirement is just as much about planning as it is dreaming of what the future holds. Taking a *balanced* approach, along with diligent savings, will provide a comfortable lifestyle free from financial stress. By not allowing yourself to be saddled with large amounts of debt enables you to save large amounts of money early, which is the key to a successful retirement. Remember Proverbs 13:11, "he grows rich who accumulates little by little"? Focus on God's way and be wise!

What Your Children Need to Be Taught about Retirement

What we teach our children about retirement and saving money is critical. God expects us to become faithful stewards by taking his resources and properly employing them to create wealth for future generations, all to the glory and advancement of God and his kingdom. Proverbs 13:22 states, "The good man bequeaths his heritage to his children's children, the wealth of the sinner is stored up for the virtuous."

If we are expected to create wealth for future generations, we must realize the need to pass on to our children the necessary knowledge and wisdom to properly develop the needed character to handle the responsibilities that such wealth requires. To an untrained steward, receiving such wealth without possessing the necessary knowledge and wisdom will most likely create a steward that is incapable of properly handling wealth. Ecclesiasticus (Sirach) 4:17–22 provides great guidance in character development and the attainment of the needed wisdom to handle inheritance stating:

> If he trusts himself to her he will inherit her, and his descendents will remain in possession of her; for though she takes him at first through winding ways, bringing fear and faintness on him, plaguing him with her discipline until she can trust him, and testing him with her ordeals, in the end she will lead him back to the straight road, and reveal her secrets to him. If he wanders away she will abandon him over to his fate.

You must teach your children about the magic of compound interest. Most children are mesmerized by "magic." Compound interest *is* magic. Compound interest must be taught in such a way that they will *never* forget its power! You must teach them that a wise person will *collect* compound interest and a foolish one will *pay* it! Demonstrate to them, in ways they understand (such as pennies doubling), what *compounding* means.

Fully Funded Retirement—In Review

The key to successful retirement lies in mastering the concept of compound interest. By starting investing early and by consistent saving and utilizing a balanced approach to investing (utilizing all investment type vehicles), you will have a successful retirement. You need to do these diligently! Setting retirement goals, seeking professional assistance, and praying for guidance about your future will guide you along the path to ensure that you end up where God intended.

Scriptures to live by:

> Matthew 13:4–9 (Sowing on fertile ground will provide biblical increase.)
>
> Ecclesiasticus (Sirach) 29:11 (Investing God's way will prove more profitable than gold.)

Proverbs 13:18 (Rejecting discipline will lead to poverty.)

Proverbs 13:11 (A sudden fortune often dwindles away; a person grows wealthy a little at a time.)

Proverbs 11:1 (God loves a just balance.)

STEP #7—PAY OFF MORTGAGE

After paying off all debt and properly funding your retirement, then we will be able to focus on what is often the single biggest debt most people have: their mortgage. Everyone knows what a mortgage is because almost everyone has one.

The sheer size of this debt for most people is reason enough to make this step #7. All through the previous six steps, we have discussed the planning and allocation of your income. Now before we tackle the biggest debt most people have, I want to take some time and explain the various aspects of mortgages.

A mortgage is debt. Ecclesiasticus (Sirach) 21:8–9 states, "To build your house on other people's money is like collecting stones for your own tomb."

Most people, upon hearing this passage, quickly get the point of the scripture. This is a very ominous

warning about going into debt to obtain a house. I believe it is important to keep this passage in mind when looking to buy a home.

If you are in the process of shopping to buy a home, you may want to think seriously about how you are going about doing it. Most people do not properly plan before buying a house, and it turns out to be a curse rather than a blessing. It is easy to buy a house; it is much more difficult to keep it. Some of the questions you want to think about before you buy a house are:

> *"Property quickly come by at first will not be blessed in the end." Proverbs* 20:21

Question #1: Do you have at least 20 percent of the value of the home saved? This means if the house is a $200,000 house, then you need to have $40,000 saved. If the answer to this question is no, then you should delay buying a home.

I understand there are many programs available to buy a home with far less down than that, but understand that the people selling the home do not care about your financial future. They care about selling a home and getting paid. There are even programs that have you pay nothing down. I understand these can be appealing, but reconsider.

Question #2: Do you already have debt before buying a house? If you do, I encourage you to strongly consider delaying the purchase of your house until you have cleaned up your debt problem before you buy.

I have seen realtors, mortgage people, loan officers, and many others involved in the process of buying a house encourage the prospective buyers to go out and obtain credit cards for the purpose of building a credit history and then using this history to qualify and obtain bigger mortgages than they might otherwise need.

This is horrible advice. If you are remotely unclear as to what God's position is on debt, you need to stop, put a bookmark on this page and re-read, study, and let it soak into your heart and mind step #4—eliminating debt!

Once you have acquired the proper mindset on debt, you will be ready to begin the process of buying a home. Often, when counseling people on buying a home, I tell them that this can be a two- to five-year process (depending upon their situation).

Most people lack the needed discipline to properly prepare, that is why a vast majority of Americans are in the financial condition they are in. My point is that the message is not what people want to hear most of the time. Consider Proverbs 20:21, "Property quickly come by at first will not be blessed in the end."

The real issue is that people are not willing to practice delayed gratification. We have become an instant-gratification society. Look at how we deal with our computers. If searching for information that you are unable to access immediately you become impatient and frustrated. Another example, the nightly news, is delivered in a series of fast-paced mini sound and

video bites. Surely, you have noticed how the finance industry markets itself to us? Television commercials are constantly bombarding us to buy "stuff" on credit; no money down; free financing for six months; skip payments; buy it now, you deserve it today, pay for it tomorrow; no job, no credit, bad credit, no problem! Where does this insanity end?

The true significance of Proverbs 20:21 is that in order to receive the blessings that God intends for all of us, we must prepare to receive those. Our heart, mind, and soul needs to be properly prepared.

Question #3: Is this house the one that I (we) need or want? Is it the house for me (us)? Often there isn't a clear answer for this question, but if it is a house that is wanted, more than needed, you must reconsider and act with caution.

The biggest mistake made by people buying houses is that it becomes an emotional decision, not a sound, logical one, grounded in wisdom; for instance, buying a house that has three or four bedrooms, and you are not married, or are married and have no children. There may be some great reasons, that a person needs that many rooms, but you must ask yourself the question, "Is it needed or wanted?"

Another big mistake involves people who make decisions based on the payment. The realtor, mortgage person, or loan officer inquires as to what you can afford. Then he structures the mortgage product and loan around that. This is not the wisest thing to do for the most expensive purchase that most people will make in their lifetime.

If you need to creatively structure your financing in order to qualify for your house (interest-only type loan) or band-aid-type products, you are either not ready, or about to make a very bad decision. If you are unable to practice the previous six steps (budgeting, tithing, paying yourself first, debt elimination, emergency fund, funding for retirement) faithfully, you are either, once again, not ready, or about to make a bad decision, financially.

If you are unmarried and/or living together, I would never recommend buying a house jointly under any circumstances! The reason being you are not married! It is sinful to live together and not be married. You *cannot* expect to prosper if you are living in sin—period! Society teaches that such thinking is old-fashioned and that there is no problem with living together. Living together is a way to "test" the relationship without having the marriage "commitment." If you are not compatible, then there is no harm in splitting up. The marriage "covenant," on the other hand, binds a man and woman together for life. God meant this covenant to provide complete safety in commitment to one another. Buying a home together outside the marriage covenant has the *potential* to entangle both, but often one more than another, in financial problems.

I do not recall ever meeting a couple (who were not married) purchasing a home together thinking they would *not* remain together forever. When the relationship fails (for whatever reason), one person is left saddled with a home they can no longer afford

and insufficient resources to succeed in keeping it. Likewise, I have yet to counsel a couple that followed this advice (not buying a home together while unmarried) and suffered for it.

There is a clear process that the Bible outlines pertaining to obtaining "blessed property." My question to you is this: "Do you want your house to be a blessing or a curse?" I have yet to find anyone who answers the question, "Ah, yes, I want it to be a curse!" Inevitably, people find themselves in deep financial problems and have no idea what caused them.

Remember the scripture at the beginning of the book, Ecclesiastes 7:29–30?

The part about God making us simple and that man's problems are of his own devising?

Did you really let that soak in? Avoid the problems, seek God's way, and live blessed!

If you are wise, you will give great weight to this wisdom and follow these processes closely. I have yet to encounter someone who did, and later regretted it.

Keep in mind Proverbs 24:27; it reads, "On open ground, plan what you have to do, make your preparation in the field; then you may go and build your house."

Your budget will act as your road map/plan. Your actions toward how you handle debt and save for your purchase are your preparation of the fields. Then you will be ready and blessed to buy a house. God will guide you to that "special" house. The one that will truly be a blessing.

Proverbs 15:19 states, "The way of the lazy is

strewn with thorns, the path of the industrious is a broad highway."

This proverb paints in my mind a very clear picture of a process to "blessed property." Taking shortcuts in preparations to buying a house will often provide a very "off-road" adventure. If you are the type that enjoys the "off-road" lifestyle—a lifestyle of bumps, gullies, pits, and cliffs, then by all means feel free to engage in these follies. If you would rather have a smooth, safe, and blessed journey, then take the time and prepare correctly. Your life's road will be a broad highway.

I find it quite useful to keep in mind, when reading Scripture, who wrote the various books that I am studying. For instance, Proverbs was written almost entirely by King Solomon. He is credited with creating more than 3,500 proverbs. He remains undoubtedly the wisest and wealthiest individual to have ever lived.

If you believe the Scriptures to be true, then read 1 Kings 3:4–15. These passages describe in detail God's gift to Solomon. In particular, verses 12–14, "I give you a heart wise and shrewd as none before you has had and none will have after you. What you have not asked I shall give you too; such riches and glory as no other king ever had."

Kings, queens, princes, governors, and the most influential people of the times would travel months, sometimes years, and pay Solomon great sums of money, in the form of gifts of gold, jewels, and priceless artifacts, to gain audience and hear his wisdom applied.

After reading such passages, I ask myself the questions: Should I be closely studying his works? Should I pay close attention to these scriptures, even if I do not yet understand them, or maybe, I do not fully agree with them? The answer is, of course, yes!

My first in-depth study of the Scriptures focused on the "wisdom books." I felt, after being homeless that I lacked the sense of wisdom. If I could gain some level of wisdom, everything else would fall into place. The books of wisdom include the books of Job, Proverbs, Ecclesiastes, Ecclesiasticus (Sirach), and Wisdom. Also grouped with the wisdom books is Song of Songs, because of its connection to Solomon. I spent many hours reading and re-reading these passages. I sought to burn them into my mind and heart.

If I were to ever obtain my dream of buying a house, I would need to be granted some discernment (wisdom). I found great comfort in Proverbs 1:1–7:

> The proverbs of Solomon son of David, king of Israel: for learning what wisdom and discipline are, for understanding words of deep meaning, for acquiring an enlightened attitude of mind—virtue, justice and fair dealing; for teaching sound judgment to the ignorant, and knowledge and sense to the young; for perceiving the meaning of proverbs and obscure sayings, the sayings of the sages and their riddles. Let the wise listen and he will learn yet more, and the man of discernment

will acquire the art of guidance. The fear of Yahweh is the beginning of knowledge; fools spurn wisdom and discipline.

Once I knew what I needed, I began to ceaselessly pray for wisdom, knowledge, and understanding. To this day, I ask daily for these gifts. I feel this has truly benefited me and my family immeasurably.

What happens if you have learned of this wisdom too late? What are you supposed to do if you find yourself in one of the situations mentioned in the previous pages?

Should you find yourself realizing that you are in the midst of a large problem, do not lose heart. You must first understand *all* of the facts. What does the full picture look like? The most important thing you can do is take action, but do not procrastinate. No problem ever went away by ignoring it. By answering the following questions, you can provide valuable guidance to your problem(s):

1. Is your problem solely an income problem? Or is it a spending problem. Or a combination of the two?

2. Does your house payment (mortgage + taxes + insurance + utilities) exceed 36 percent of your net income (take-home pay)?

3. Are the problems you have been experiencing, or are beginning to experience, long term or short term in nature? What I mean by this is, are the problems short-term problems, or do you honestly foresee them continuing

well into the future? You must be very honest when answering this question.

4. What steps can you take today to begin fixing your situation?

I want to discuss a number of possible answers to these questions:

1. If your problem is an income problem, a spending problem or a combination of the two, your solution is relatively simple. Earn more income, cut your spending, or wiser yet, do both!

2. If your mortgage payment (the combination of your payment, insurance, taxes, and utilities exceed 36 percent of your net income (take-home pay) you are living in a place that is too expensive.

Keep in mind, the cost of a house, condo, apartment, or other dwelling you may purchase involves not only the payment you make to the mortgage company each month, but other costs that, when added in, begin the financial descent into trouble. These overlooked additional costs might include maintenance and repair of the property.

Is your property older? What types of repairs might the property need? Is your property new? What types of furnishings will it require? Landscaping? Homeowner's fees or dues required by associations? If your costs are above 36 percent of your net income, you will most always struggle, if not eventually drown, financially. The answer here is: If your costs are too high, either increase your income (long term) or cut costs. Better yet, strongly consider selling and moving to a more affordable place.

Many people, when faced with realization of a possible move, think of fifty reasons why they should not move. They justify in their mind that what they are doing is not the problem. A wise person will consider *all* options.

3. If the problems you are having, or beginning to have, are truthfully short-term problems, then maybe short-term solutions are the answer. If they are long term, you must be much more careful to understand the issue(s) and address the long-term issue(s) properly.

It is never a good idea to address a long-term problem with a short-term solution. The key here is having a keen ability to recognize: Is this a short-term issue or a long-term issue? How much control do you have over what is occurring? How much control do you have over the economy or health issues? If you answer this honestly, your answer should be close to something like zero! Seek wise counsel, and unceasingly pray!

4. The actions you take, or don't take, will be as critical as the problems themselves. No matter what the situation, do something! If you have no idea how to address the problem(s), seek help. The only shame will be found in the person who does or says nothing. Proverbs

13:20 states, "Make the wise your companions and you grow wise yourself." Proverbs 19:20 says, "Listen to advice, accept correction, to be the wiser to come."

Both of these proverbs stress seeking wisdom from people who are wiser than yourself, and you will derive the benefit of their wisdom not only for the immediate but for the future as well.

Mentioned earlier was the concept of delayed gratification. The concept is an incredibly powerful tool that should be used often, especially with *all* large purchases.

What Delayed Gratification Can Do for You!

In a previous chapter (Step #6) I mentioned the concept of delayed gratification. Let me explain what can be accomplished through delayed gratification. I want to walk through a financial scenario that shows two families: family A and family B. This exercise powerfully demonstrates the principle of delayed gratification, in the purchase of a home. We will look at the financial decisions of both families, and I will let you decide which family is the better financial steward.

Family A and family B are ready to buy their dream homes (you will find it helpful to refer to the illustration I have provided at the end of this example). The homes are priced identically at $300,000. Family A and family B will put down identical down payments of $30,000 (please note: the $30,000 down payment represents a 10 percent down payment not

the 20 percent I recommend). Both obtain mortgages at an 8.5 percent, and both are given thirty-year terms. Both are looking at monthly payments of approximately $2,100 (neither of these families' payments include taxes or insurance).

Family A buys their "dream" home under this scenario. Family B, however, decides to wait on obtaining their dream home and instead purchases a home that fits their needs instead of their desires (*delayed gratification*). Family B decides to purchase a $150,000 home for now. They still put $30,000 or 20 percent of the mortgage down, and still obtain a thirty-year mortgage at 8.5 percent (the same as family A). The difference is that family A has a balance of $270,000 and takes thirty years to pay off the mortgage. Family B in the meantime has a mortgage balance of only $120,000. Family B still makes the $2,100 payment (plus taxes and home owner's insurance) on their mortgage just as if they were living in their dream home. At this rate, family B will pay off its mortgage in six years and two months.

They now have a home fully paid for that has appreciated (most likely) somewhat, in value. Then, family B sells their current home and buys their dream home.

For argument's sake, and simplicity, let's say they recouped what they paid for the house ($154,360). They then buy the $300,000 dream home (just like family A). To keep this comparison real, we will pretend that the cost of the dream home has increased to

$350,000. They now put the proceeds of their home sale ($155,000–please note this is rounded up for simplicity purposes) as the down payment for their dream home. They now have a thirty-year mortgage with a balance of $195,000. They continue making $2,100 payments. Family B will have their dream home paid off in roughly thirteen years and four months. After family B pays off their dream home, they begin to use what used to be their mortgage payment ($2,100) and invest it. Let's say they receive 8 percent return from their investing. Family B will continue investing for eleven years and two months. Remember, family B took six years and two months to pay off their first mortgage and twelve years and eight months to pay off their second mortgage—a total of eighteen years and ten months.

After thirty years, let's look at the situation of both families; family A was paying the same payment as family B ($2,100 each month). Both families, after thirty years, own their "dream homes," and both have 100 percent equity in their respective homes (both homes are now worth $600,000 after thirty years). Family A ended up paying $747,383 for their home (principal of $270,000 and interest of $477,383). Family B ended up paying $319,069 for an identical "dream home" (principal of $195,000 and interest of $124,069). I think you would agree that the better financial steward is obvious; family B in a landslide!

Let's do a side by side on the numbers:

THOMAS E. ZORDANI

	Family A	Family B
Cost of First Home	$300,000	$150,000
Down Payment	- $30,000	- $30,000
Balance of Loan	$270,000	$120,000
Monthly Payment (approx)	$2,100	$2,100
Loan Terms (30 years at 8.5%)	yes	yes
Cost of Principal	$270,000	$120,000 (first house)
Cost of Interest	$477,383	$34,360 (first house)
Total Cost of Loans	$747,383	$154,360 (first house)
Cost of Second Home	-	$350,000
Down Payment	-	$155,000
Balance of Loan	-	$195,000
Monthly Payment	-	$2,100
Loan Terms (30 years at 8.5%)	-	yes
Cost of Principal	-	$195,000 (second house)
Cost of Interest	-	$124,069 (second house)
Total Cost of Loans	-	$319,069 (second house)

Summary

	Family A	Family B
Cost of Principal	$270,000	$120,000 (first house)
	-	$195,000 (second house)
	$270,000	$315,000
Cost of Interest	$477,383	$34,360 (first house)
	-	$124,069 (second house)
	$477,383	$158,429
Total Cost of Loans	$270,000	$315,000
	$477,383	$158,429
	$747,383	$473,429 (both houses)
Net Difference		+ $273,954

Family B comes out $273,954 ahead of family A by practicing delayed gratification!

However, we are not quite done with the comparison. Remember family B finished purchasing their "dream home" eleven years and 2 months before family A. Keep in mind both had identical monthly mortgage payments of $2,100. Also, remember that family B then used what used to go to the mortgage payment, and invested it.

After eleven years and 2 months family B will have accumulated an additional $423,080 in investments (before tax). The difference is really $697,034! Now if family B was really smart, and we know they were, they will have invested their money in a tax-never investment vehicle so as to limit the taxes owed on the future income. Do not forget that we had family B break even on their first deal. If we had the house appreciating like most homes do, the numbers are actually substantially larger. Now, which family is truly the better financial steward?

Paying Off Your Mortgage

I have discussed preparing to buy a house and the pitfalls to avoid when buying a house, and what it is that delayed gratification can accomplish when making large purchases. I want now to discuss paying off what is typically the single largest debt that most people have–their home mortgage. I will discuss a number of scenarios. Please note: family B (in the previous example) did not use any of the strategies I will be discussing in this chapter.

I want to continue using the income level I have used throughout the book ($4,000 / month, or $48,000 / year). Let's suppose a particular family bought a home before reading this book. The family was *told* that it is qualified for a $200,000 home (by society's standards). Let's also suppose this is the family's first home and it qualifies for a zero-down-payment program (not uncommon). Let's also suppose that the loan it obtains is a 30-year mort-

gage at 6.5 percent. The monthly payment would be something like $1,264. This fits comfortably into society's *measure* of what can be afforded, what this particular family is *qualified* to borrow, based on its debt-to-income-ratio. Let's be honest about another fact—- that is that, people often obtain a house, and then go out and acquire other debt (cars, credit cards etc...).

What is not taken into account with this scenario that when the taxes and insurance of this $200,000 home are taken into account, the payment becomes closer to $1,486 (I am using $75 / month in taxes and $54 / month for home owner's insurance and $84 for mortgage insurance costs as an average. It *MUST* be understood that these expenses may be considerably higher or lower, based upon where you live). This is still within the guidelines of *qualifying* this family for the mortgage, but it is at the upper limit of 36 percent ($4,000 / month income x .36 = $1,440 monthly payment).

What makes this scenario a problem lurking in the weeds is that the other costs of the home will be what make this family begin the descent into financial trouble. What do I mean by this? There are additional costs to owning the home (I have mentioned some of these costs previously). These are costs associated with maintenance, upkeep, utilities, and the furnishing of the home. When all of these factors are added together, given time, this family will find itself in a financial mess!

Let's suppose the family had read this book before

it bought the house and that had heeded the advice. The family would then realize that the $200,000 home is more expensive than they can afford. The family should find one that costs $180,000. The difference that the $20,000 makes is the difference between a blessing and a curse! The payment for an $180,000 home is $1,138. When the taxes and insurance are added into the payment it becomes $1,350, still under the limit of 36 percent of $1,440.

Now, I would like to demonstrate a couple of options (choices) based on this family's scenario. First, the family could afford the $200,000 if it practiced delayed gratification, i.e. waited the appropriate time until outstanding debts have been eliminated and saved the recommended 20 percent down ($40,000) for the down-payment ($36,000 down-payment for the $180,000 home).

If this family had followed this advice then the payment on the $200,000 would be $1,266 / month ($1,137 of principal and interest, $75 / month taxes and $54 / month / home owner's insurance). Please note, because this family put 20 percent down, it is not required to have mortgage insurance. If the family purchased the $180,000 home, placing 20 percent down the payments would be $1,039 ($910 of principal and interest, $75 / month taxes and $54 / month / home owner's insurance). This number is well under the 36 percent of $1,440! These numbers will make a BIG difference in long-term financial health.

Let's examine some strategies involved in paying off your home altogether—and sooner! First, and most often used, is paying additional money each month, or making additional payments during the course of the year. If an additional $100 / month is paid, 5 years and 7 months of payments will be removed from a 30 year mortgage and $55,956 in interest will have been saved on a $200,000 loan! On a $180,000 loan $54,458 in interest will have been saved, and 6 years and 1 month will have been removed from a 30 year mortgage!

If a 20 percent down-payment is made on the $200,000 home, the numbers and savings will be identical to the scenario above, for the $180,000 home. If a 20 percent down-payment on the $180,000 home is made, plus an extra payment of $100 / month, the savings would total $51,087, and would shorten the length of the 30 year mortgage by 7 years and 2 months!

Now, let's examine a little-used alternative,— a bi-weekly payment. A $180,000 mortgage ($200,000 home with 20 percent down) requires a payment of $1,137 (principal and interest only). If a bi-weekly payment is made, the current payment required would be $568.50 (please note: banks and lenders calculate bi-weekly payments as 2 payments / month, not payments every two weeks–in my opinion this is truly a semi-monthly schedule— $1,137 / 2 = $568.50). By making a bi-weekly payment (1/2 of your original payment 2 times / month), $54,593 of interest will be saved, and 7 years removed from a 30 year mortgage. The reason that this works as it does, is because when a ½ payment is made on a mortgage (twice a month),

the amount of compounding interest that accrues is almost cut in half (thus utilizing a principle of "the rule of 72" in your favor–time).

Keeping in mind Proverbs 11:1 (balance) If this family had utilized *both* alternatives (extra payment amounts and bi-weekly payments) it would save $110,320 in interest, and would cut almost 13 years from the 30 year mortgage. These two simple changes ($100 of extra income and simply changing the way the mortgage is paid) will make an enormous difference! Is this not prudent stewardship?

What Your Children Need to Know about Owning a Home

Most people aspire to owning their own dwelling whether it is a house, condo, or an apartment. Teaching children about owning a home someday is a very important. Teaching your children how to buy it *correctly* is even more important. Children need to learn the proper handling of money, so that when the day comes to purchase their first home, it is a blessing and not a curse. You must impart to them that it is not necessary to possess credit cards to purchase a home. If you properly prepare for buying a home, God will bless you. Children must be taught that *it is easy* to buy a home, whether you are properly prepared or not; however, *keeping* the home is entirely a different matter, and much more difficult.

Teach your children about "delayed gratification." This powerful principle should be taught to the very young. Children struggle with waiting. Today's soci-

ety, on the other hand, teaches *instant* gratification. Delayed gratification, when learned and practiced in many situations, and on *all* large purchases, will save thousands—perhaps tens of thousands, even hundreds of thousands, of dollars, for the person who persistently practices it.

Paying Off the Mortgage—In Review

God provides a clear path in preparation for the purchase of a home. He wants it to be a blessing and not a curse. He wants that we should seek his guidance when purchasing a home. Obey these practices: You should have saved at least 20 percent of the purchase price.

1. To properly prepare for the purchase of a home, you should not have any other debt.

2. Do not buy a home that is beyond your ability to pay. Just because you *qualify* for a more expensive home does not mean you should *buy* it. You should focus on buying a home that you "need" not a home that you "want." I do not know any people who have found themselves in financial trouble because they said "no" to buying a more expensive home.

3. Utilize the principle of compounding by making bi-weekly mortgage payments and

additional principal payments–it will save you thousands!

4. Never buy a home together with your "significant other" if you are not married. This can lead to all sorts of problems.

It is impossible to predict the future, but you can better be prepared for whatever may happen. Having sufficient income saved and owning a home that fits well into your financial budget will prove wise. Practicing delayed gratification in the purchase of a home will pay for itself many times over.

Scriptures to live by:

Ecclesiasticus (Sirach) 21:8–9 (Using borrowed money to obtain your home is like collecting stones for your own tomb.)

Proverbs 20:21 (Property that is acquired quickly will not be blessed property—prepare!)

Proverbs 24:27 (Plan what you have to do, then go and build your house.)

Proverbs 13:20 (Follow wise counsel and you yourself will grow wise.)

STEP #8—GIVE AND SAVE IN ABUNDANCE

The eighth and final step in changing your financial future is mastering giving and perfecting saving. The previous step that discussed giving (step #2) and saving (steps #3, #5, and #6) professed minimal levels of action. The levels of action set forth in this step are difficult for some people to comprehend. Can you imagine giving away 50–75 percent of everything you make? Can you imagine saving 25–50 percent of everything you make? Aligning yourself with God's ways and principles makes this possible.

A constant message throughout Scripture, pertaining to finance, is that God is a God of abundance and prosperity. God wishes that we enjoy fully in his abundance and prosperity. It is our humanity that complicates God's plans for us. By operating outside of God's ways, we stifle the abundance and prosperity that is rightfully ours.

God wants us to have abundance, prosperity, and blessing in all that we undertake. Consider Leviticus 26:3–6.

> If you live according to my laws, if you keep my commandments and put them into practice, I will give you the rain you need at the right time; the earth shall give its produce and the trees of the countryside their fruits; you shall thresh until vintage time and gather grapes until sowing time. You shall eat your fill of bread and live secure in your land.

Leviticus 26:9–10 states:

> I will give peace to the land, and you shall sleep with none to frighten you. I will turn toward you, I will make you fruitful and multiply, and I will uphold my Covenant with you. You shall eat your fill of last year's harvest, and throw out the old to make room for the new.

The message is unmistakably clear within the two related passages. If you follow the ways of God, if you obey, you will prosper. It does not say, "If you obey my laws and commandments, I will *consider* blessing you." God promises an abundance and prosperity so full that we will be unable to accommodate it.

Consider the last sentence of Leviticus 26:9–10, "You shall eat your fill, you will throw out the old to make room for the new." This promises not only

"To receive blessings, you must first give, and then have faith!"

will you have enough in *every* way, but you will constantly have to discard the old to make room for the new. Are you prepared for this?

We are often uncomfortable parting with possessions, large or small. It is as if we will lose something that cannot be replaced. The reasons are many, but in most instances, our actions betray us by demonstrating that we lack faith. God is promising he will replace old things with new. He will provide! Genesis 9:1 also portrays a message of prosperity and abundance by saying, "As for you, be fruitful and multiply, teem over the earth and be lord of it."

There is no doubt God provided us with such potential abundance that we could spread out, multiply, teem over the earth, and rule it. It did not say there is only a "little" of everything, so use it sparingly; or stake out your "small" share before it is gone; or you deserve a "little," so don't expect much! The Bible constantly reinforces the promise that in order to receive blessings, you must first give, and then have faith!

A person first must give (sow) before he/she can reap (experience increase); it must be understood how "sowing and reaping" works.

A farmer is never able to reap his crop before he has sown it. You can never expect to reap something other than what has been sown. This means that if you sow wheat, you can never expect to harvest corn. Likewise, if you sow a crop of wheat thinly, you cannot expect to harvest that same field abundant with wheat. If you sow abundantly, you will receive abun-

dantly. You cannot give "little" and expect to receive much.

This principle works equally for good and bad, which means, if you sow malice, you will reap malice. If you sow love, you will receive love. You cannot sow bad and reap good, nor sow good and reap bad.

Expecting to receive and then give, does not work. This violates the universal principle of "sowing and reaping" also known as the "law of reciprocity." Many people think that "promising" to give, if they receive, replaces having to give before you receive. It doesn't!

You cannot just "think" about giving or "hope" to give after you have been given. You must actively seek to give. You must plan to give. You must "trust" and have "faith" in God's promises. Give with no reservation or doubt that "all" of your needs will be addressed.

In Galatians 6:7–10, St. Paul taught sowing and reaping by saying:

> Don't delude yourself into thinking God can be cheated: where a man sows, there he reaps; if he sows in the field of self-indulgence he will get a harvest of corruption out of it; if he sows in the field of the Spirit he will get from it a harvest of eternal life. We must never get tired of doing good because if we don't give up the struggle we shall get our harvest at the proper time. While we have the chance, we must do good to all, and especially to our brothers in the faith.

There are a great number of passages that specifically relate to the principles of "sowing and reaping" and "prosperity and abundance." The catch lies in the adherence to the law of "reciprocity."

All of these principles (prosperity, abundance, sowing and reaping) are contained within the three major principles mentioned at the beginning of this book; sowing lies within giving, reaping within increase, prosperity lies within management; and abundance lies within increase.

Christ understood that we worry about giving. We worry that if we give "too" much, we will not have enough to meet our needs. He is gentle but firm in reminding us that God the Father knows what we need, and he promises to provide it.

Matthew 6:25–34 says:

> That is why I am telling you not to worry about your life and what you are to eat, nor about your body and how you are to clothe it. Surely life means more than food, and the body more than clothing! Look at the birds in the sky. They do not sow or reap or gather into barns; yet your heavenly Father feeds them. Are you not worth much more than they are? Can any of you, for all his worrying, add one single cubit to his span of life? And why worry about clothing? Think of the flowers growing in the fields; they never have to work or spin; yet I assure you that not even Solomon in all his regalia was robed like one of these. Now if that is how God clothes the grass in the field which is there today and thrown into the furnace tomorrow, will he not much more

look after you, you men of little faith? So do not worry, do not say, "What are we to eat? What are we to drink? How are we to be clothed?" It is the pagans who set their hearts on all these things. Your heavenly Father knows you need them all. Set your hearts on his kingdom first, and on his righteousness, and all of these other things will be given you as well. So do not worry about tomorrow: tomorrow will take care of itself. Each day has enough trouble of its own.

The passage of Matthew is clear: worry does nothing to help. It actually hinders us from relying upon God. It prevents us from relying upon God by weakening our faith. We must have 100 percent confidence and trust that God will provide for us in *every* way!

Remember 2 Corinthians 9:6–9 in the chapter on tithing, "Do not forget: thin sowing means thin reaping; the more you sow the more you reap ... abundant blessings"? The concluding lines of that passage were omitted. We must examine this particular passage in its full context. Continued, 2 Corinthians 9:10–12, where it states:

> As scripture says *He was free in almsgiving, and gave to the poor: his good deeds will never be forgotten.* "The one who provides *seed for the sower and bread for food* will provide you with all the seed you want and make *the harvest of your good deeds* a larger one, and made richer in every way, you will be able to do all the generous things which, through us, are the cause of thanksgiving to God.

This passage makes a definite promise of God's blessing to those who give, give freely and give abundantly. *"Made richer in every way"* clearly sets the bar very high, with the abundance, we can expect to receive from this promise.

Jesus spoke powerfully on "giving" in the parable of the widow's mite (money) stating:

> As he looked up he saw rich people putting their offerings into the treasury; then he happened to notice a poverty-stricken widow putting in two small coins, and he said, "I tell you truly, this poor widow has put in more than any of them; for these have contributed money they had over, but she from the little she had has put in all she had to live on."
>
> Luke 8:1–4

Keep in mind that if you cannot give, God understands; if you can give and don't, God knows! [19]

Other passages speak specifically to "giving," the rewards and benefits of "giving," as well as the opposite (giving too little or not giving at all) and the implications of "not giving" due to pride, fear, and selfishness, and their consequences. Let's first look at giving.

Giving

The Apostle Paul spoke of the joy of giving by quoting Jesus, in Acts 20:35, saying, "I did this to show you that this is how we must exert ourselves to support the weak, remembering the words of the Lord Jesus, who himself said, 'There is more happiness in giving than in receiving.'"

An impressive act of "offering" is found in Scripture in the story of Zacchaeus in Luke 19:1–10:

> He entered Jericho and was going through the town when a man whose name was Zacchaeus made his appearance; he was one of the senior tax collectors and a wealthy man. He was anxious to see what kind of man Jesus was, but he was too short and could not see him for the crowd; so he ran ahead and climbed a sycamore tree to catch a glimpse of Jesus who was to pass that way. When Jesus reached the spot he looked up and spoke to him: "Zacchaeus, come down. Hurry, because I must stay at your house today." And he hurried

and welcomed him joyfully. They all complained when they saw what was happening. "He has gone to stay at a sinner's house," they said. But Zucchaeus stood his ground and said to the Lord, "Look, sir, I am going to give half my property to the poor, and if I have cheated anybody I will pay him back four times the amount." And Jesus said to him, "Today salvation has come to this house, because this man too is a son of Abraham; for the Son of Man has come to seek out and save what was lost."

Zacchaeus' life was instantly transformed from his meeting with Christ. He decided at that time to give away half of everything he owned (a large sum). He was a very wealthy man. You need to think about the implications of why Zacchaeus gave away half his wealth. Was he concerned about his own salvation? One thing is certain, Zacchaeus had been changed and his salvation earned at that moment.

Scripture is clear. We are expected to give. Giving needs to be looked at from the perspective of not only monetary giving, but in actions of kindness and humility with those less fortunate. The rewards for operating in this manner are profound. God promises that he will not be outdone in giving.

There are three types of giving. The first is tithing; the second, offerings; the third is alms-giving. Since we have already discussed tithing in step #2, we will focus on offerings and alms-giving.

Alms-giving is a form of giving to atone for sin or our sinful nature. Alms are always given to the poor and are more penitent if done in secret (the identity of the giver is only known to God). God holds a special place in his heart for the weak, infirmed, and poor. He expects us to come to their aid and provide for them generously.

Ecclesiasticus (Sirach) 4:1–11.

My son, do not refuse the poor a livelihood, do not tantalize the needy. Do not add to the sufferings of the hungry, do not bait a man in distress. Do not aggravate the heart already angry, nor keep the destitute waiting for your alms. Do not repulse a hard-pressed beggar, nor turn your face from a poor man. Do not avert your eyes from the destitute, give no man occasion to curse you; for if a man curses you in the bitterness of his soul, his maker will hear his imprecation. Gain the love of the community, bow your head to a man of authority. To the poor man lend an ear, and return his greeting courteously. Save the oppressed from the hand of the oppressor, and do not be mean-spirited in your judgments. Be like a father to orphans, and as good as a husband to widows. And you will be like a son to the Most High, whose love for you will surpass your mother's.

Ecclesiasticus (Sirach) 12:1–2, "If you do a good turn, know for whom you are doing it, and your good deed will not go to waste. Do good to a devout man, and you will receive a reward, if not from him, then certainly the Most High."

Another form of giving is "offering." An offering is a gift to honor God and is over and above tithing. It is not possible to make an "offering" if you do not tithe. An impressive form of offering is found in 2 Corinthians 8:1–5.

> Now here, brothers, is the news of the grace of God which was given in the churches in Macedonia; and of how, throughout great trials by suffering, their constant cheerfulness and their intense poverty have overflowed in a wealth of generosity. I can swear that they gave not only as much as they could afford, but far more, and quite spontaneously, begging and begging us for the favor of sharing this service to the saints and what was quite unexpected, they offered their own selves first to God and, under God, to us.

The Christians of Macedonia, impoverished as they were, opened their hearts and their purses in such a way that the Apostle Paul was filled with awe at the generosity of the congregation. Paul used this opportunity to challenge the church at Corinth to continue funding "works of mercy" in such a way as Macedonia had. Paul drove this point home when he stated in 2 Corinthians 8:9–15:

> Remember how generous the Lord Jesus was: he was rich, but he became poor for your sake, to make you rich out of his poverty. As I say, I am only making a suggestion; it is only fair to you, since you were the first, a year ago, not only in taking action but even in deciding to. So now finish the work and let the results be worthy, as far as you can afford it, of the decision you made so promptly. As long as the readiness is there, a man is acceptable with whatever he can afford; never mind what is beyond his means. This does not

mean that to give relief to others you ought to make things difficult for yourselves: it is a question of balancing what happens to be your surplus now against their present need, and one day they may have something to spare that will supply your own need. That is how we strike a balance: as scripture says: *The man who gathered much had none too much, the man who gathered little did not go short.*

You can become a much more effective giver if you are willing to make three life-changing commitments:

1. Commit yourself to honoring God with your life; your life will be filled with profound purpose and meaning. Daily study of Scripture will contribute to your spiritual enlightenment, which in turn contributes to character development. Character is the keystone to becoming a "true" steward and obtaining true wealth. No amount of wealth has the ability to set you free if you suffer from poverty of character!

2. Commit yourself to honoring God by discovering why he has chosen to supply you with more financial resources than you need. Often, this is a character test. Christ was amazingly accurate when he stated that your heartstrings are attached securely to your purse strings. God expects you to give so that you can receive so that you can give more so that you can give again.

3. Commit yourself to honoring God with your wealth; understand that God owns everything that exists, including your wealth. We are merely stewards of it. Commit to understand that God will often test your heart in sharing with people less fortunate than yourself. Nothing is better at revealing your true character than the uses to which you employ your money (reference Matthew 6:19–21). [20]

Lack of Giving?

Scripture lays out clear consequences if we turn away from what we should be doing and when we have the ability to give and don't, or profess to be givers and aren't. Christ addressed this issue when he taught on integrity.

Luke 6:43–45 professes:

> There is no sound tree that produces rotten fruit, nor again a rotten tree that produces sound fruit. For every tree can be told by its own fruit: people do not pick figs from thorns, nor gather grapes from brambles. A good man draws what is good from the store of goodness in his heart; a bad man draws what is bad from the store of badness. For a man's words flow out of what fills his heart.

Actions speak louder than words, because it is said, that we are measured by what we say, and remembered by what we do or don't do!

The Bible cautions about "not giving." Proverbs

addresses this in 21:13, which states, "He who shuts his ear to the poor man's cry shall himself plead and not be heard."

If we expect our needs to be met, we must help others meet theirs.

Matthew 19:16–22 (parable of the rich young man):

> And there was a man who came to him and asked, "Master, what good deed must I do to possess eternal life?" Jesus said to him, "Why do you ask me about what is good? There is one alone who is good. But if you wish to enter into life, keep the commandments." He said, "Which?" "These" Jesus replied, *"You must not kill. You must not commit adultery. You must not steal. You must not bring false witness. Honor your father and mother, and: you must love your neighbor as yourself."* The young man said to him, "I have kept all these. What more do I need to do?" Jesus said, "If you wish to be perfect, go and sell what you own and give the money to the poor, and you will have treasure in heaven; then come, follow me." But when the young man heard these words he went away sad, for he was a man of great wealth.

What is your attitude toward money and possessions? If you are like most, you value your money and your possessions. Do not commit the sin of pride by letting your money and possessions become your fortress. Ecclesiasticus (Sirach) 10:14 warns, "The beginning of human pride is to desert the Lord, and turn one's heart away from one's maker. Since the

beginning of pride is sin, whoever clings to it will pour forth filth."

Christ warned us of the consequences of loving money and possessions in Mark 6:24, which states: "No one can be the slave of two masters: he will either hate the first and love the second, or treat the first with respect and the second with scorn. You cannot be the slave of both God and of money." If asked to choose, what will your choice be?

Saving and Investing Abundantly

The Bible contains many passages that speak to "biblical investing" or increase. God provides an incredible abundance of resources from which we are expected to grow and multiply these resources, all to the glory of God! The problem that most people have is that they fail to see these resources or the abundance of possibilities. We are often blinded from our lack of faith.

In Luke 5:1–11, "The first four disciples are called," Peter, the apostle, was blind to the possibilities of abundance and prosperity that were in front of him.

> Now he was standing one day by the Lake of Gennesaret, with the crowd pressing around him listening to the word of God, when he caught sight of two boats close to the bank. The fisherman had gone out of them and were washing their nets. He got into one of the boats—it was Simon's—and asked him to put out a little from shore. Then he sat down and taught the crowds from the boat.

When he had finished speaking he said to Simon, "Put out into deep water and pay out your nets for a catch." "Master," Simon replied, "we worked hard all night long and caught nothing, but if you say so, I will pay out the nets." And when they had done this they netted such a huge number of fish that their nets began to tear, so he signaled to their companions in the other boat to come and help them; when these came, they filled the two boats to sinking point.

When Simon Peter saw this he fell at the knees of Jesus saying, "Leave me, Lord; I am a sinful man." For he and all his companions were completely overcome by the catch they had made; so also were James and John, sons of Zebedee, who were Simon's partners. But Jesus said to Simon, "Do not be afraid; from now on it is men that you will catch." Then, bringing their boats back to land they left everything and followed him.

I feel it is important to understand the frame of reference this story provides. It was conventional wisdom at the time that fishing was done during the night when the fish were close to the surface because the fishes' food source was at the surface. During the day, the fish sought deep water. When Jesus asked that they lower their nets during the day, Peter must have been thinking, *What? We have fished all night long, unsuccessfully. No one fishes during the day. To prove my point, I will listen to you.* To his utter astonishment, they caught so many fish that their nets began to tear. He had to call his fishing partners to assist in hauling them in. They caught so many fish that the boats began taking on water. What must Peter have been thinking at that time? He felt so ashamed of his arrogance that he deemed himself unworthy to be in the presence of Jesus. Peter's realization that, through Jesus' teachings, God's ways are not limited to man's conventional thinking. God's ways are not man's ways. We often handicap ourselves because we fail to open ourselves to God's abundance.

How much wealth do you have? This can be a very interesting question to ask yourself. One could easily throw out any potential number of monetary value, reflecting what might be contained in various bank account(s) or investment(s) at any given moment. Perhaps answer more esoterically, "I measure wealth not in money but rather in family, friends, health and good fortune," or other such things.

Look at the question again, study it, and see the possibilities. What needs to be drawn from that question is: What is your *potential* wealth? What are you *capable* of? What is the *size* of the reservoir from which you draw your resources?

Do you see the question differently now? The answer, of course, is as abundant as money itself. If you answered something less, then you need to change the way you think. God provided us with an incredible tool that is unlike any other tool in the universe—our brain. We are challenged to utilize it to the fullest.

I once attended a self-help seminar that performed an interesting exercise with the audience,

myself included. The speaker asked that we take out a sheet of paper and a pen and that we would be given one minute to write our own names as many times as we could. We were told that we could write our names however we wished, first name, last name, full name, or nickname. He yelled out, "Begin!" He notified us when there was thirty seconds left, then twenty, then fifteen, then ten, and then counted down from there nine, eight, seven... As the time ticked down, I began to feel a sense of pressure. I wrote my name forty-one times. I noticed as the time ticked down, my writing became less legible. We then all stood up. He then said, "Okay, if you have less than twenty-five, please sit down!" A few people sat down. "If you have less than fifty, please sit down!" Seventy percent of the room was now seated. "If you have less than seventy-five, please sit down!" Over 95 percent of the room was now seated.

I became curious as to who had the most and how many. He then said, "If you have less than one hundred, please sit." A few more sat down. I began to think to myself, *How is that even possible?* The winner had 365! I was astonished! I had to understand how that was even possible. What I found out was that this particular individual had attended the seminar before and was familiar with the exercise. He had written a page full of dots. Then it occurred to me: the speaker had said, "You can write your name *any* way you like." It was my line of thought that dictated how I would perform the task. I limited my abilities to a conventional way of thinking. By doing so, I limited my own performance. It was at this time that it occurred to me, how often had I limited my performances in other situations? And how about you? How often might you have limited your abundance because you thought your ways are God's ways, when in fact they aren't?

The second lesson I learned from this very simple exercise was regarding the self-imposed anxiety I experienced. The speaker did not put any undue pressure on me. He was merely counting down the time. The time would have passed had the speaker not even mentioned it. I realized that I was solely responsible for the pressure, and I was imposing it on myself. I was *choosing* to place pressure on myself to perform at my best. Actually, what was happening was that I wasn't performing anywhere near what I was capable of performing!

I can assure you that God *knows* what you are capable of. If you are willing to allow him to guide you, you will quite likely experience immense amounts of blessings and prosperity.

Now ask yourself the question: *How much wealth is there in the world?* The answer to this is the same as the earlier question, only more—infinitely more!

Because someone has a lot of money does not mean someone else does not. The person, who does not yet have it, simply needs to tap into the limitless resources that God provides and access it. Ask for it. Pray for it. Change what needs to be changed, and it will be granted to you.

People struggle to grasp this line of thinking

because we limit ourselves with a reality that we invent. And it is self-imposed, through our fears and limited scope of thinking. We constantly defeat ourselves by not daring to think big. Remember the purpose of biblical "increase" is not to pursue wealth for wealth's sake. The purpose for which you seek wealth should be to increase your "charitable giving" to glorify God and advance his kingdom!

A great parable to learn what God expects of us regarding the resources he has provided is found in Matthew. Most everyone is familiar with the parable of the talents. Matthew 25:14–30:

> It is like a man on his way abroad who summoned his servants and entrusted his property to them. To one he gave five talents, to another two, to a third one; each in proportion to his ability. Then he set out. The man who had received the five talents promptly went out and traded with them and made five more. The man who had received two made two more in the same way. But the man who received the one went off and dug a hole in the ground and hid his master's money. Now a long time after, the master of those servants came back and went through the accounts with them. The man who had received the five talents came forward bringing five more. "Sir," he said, "you entrusted me with five talents; here are five more that I have made." His master said to him, "Well done, good and faithful servant; you have shown you can be faithful in small things, I will trust you with greater; come and join in your master's happiness." Next the man with the two talents

came forward. "Sir," he said, "you entrusted me with two talents; here are two more that I have made." His master said to him, "Well done, good and faithful servant; you have shown you can be faithful in small things, I will trust you with greater; come and join your master's happiness." Last came forward the man who had the one talent. "Sir," said he, "I had heard you were a hard man, reaping where you have not sown and gathering where you have not scattered; so I was afraid and went off and hid your talent in the ground. Here it is, it was yours, you have it back." But the master answered him, "You wicked and lazy servant! So you knew that I would reap where I have not sown and gather where I have not scattered? Well then, you should have deposited my money with the bankers, and on my return I would have removed my capital with interest. So now take the talent from him and give it to the man who has ten talents. For to everyone who has will be given more, and he will have more than enough but from the man who has not, even what he has will be taken away. As for this good-for-nothing servant, throw him out into the dark, where there will be weeping and grinding of teeth."

At first this parable seems to take the opposite approach of what one might think God expects and Jesus taught. You might recall such passages as Matthew 5:3 (the Beatitudes): "Happy are the poor ... theirs is the kingdom of heaven." What most people confuse is that poor is poor in spirit, not wealth!

Perhaps you recall Matthew 19:23–26?

> Then Jesus said to his disciples, "I tell you solemnly, it will be hard for a rich man to enter the kingdom of heaven. Yes, I tell you again, it is easier for a camel to pass through the eye of a needle than for a rich man to enter the kingdom of heaven." When the disciples heard this they were astonished. "Who can be saved then?" they said. Jesus gazed at them. "For men," he told them, "This is impossible; for God everything is possible."

What many people fail to realize is that this lesson does not mean because someone is rich that they cannot enter heaven. It means that someone who "loves" riches cannot enter heaven. The love of riches is what causes sin and alienation from God. Alienation from God will cause many types of problems, especially financial problems.

Are you fearful of making the most of *all* the resources God sees fit to provide you? Do not be like the foolish servant and bury the master's wealth

Why should God supply you with abundance if you have no intention of multiplying that abundance to his glory? That is poor stewardship. Your abundance should rightfully be placed with someone who will multiply the abundance properly to God's glory.

The master gave proportionately to each servant's abilities. How do you view your ability? Have you ever stopped to think if you feel that you constantly are in need, or you do not have what you think you deserve, it might be because you lack the proper attitude to deserve more? Mastering the principle of "management" will provide the foundation to proper saving and investing God's treasure.

You cannot expect to receive five talents if you did not manage your one talent properly. You must first learn to master the management of your one talent to deserve managing the two talents, and then learn to master managing the two talents, before you will deserve to manage five talents.

Luke 16:9–13 drives this point home stating:

> And so I tell you this: use money, tainted as it is, to win you friends, and thus make sure when it fails you, they will welcome you into the tents of eternity. The man who can be trusted in little things can be trusted in great; the man who is dishonest in little things will be dishonest in great. If then you cannot be trusted with money, that tainted thing, who will trust you with genuine riches? And if you cannot be trusted with what is not yours, who will give you what is your very own?

Trust in God

How much do you trust in God? If it is anything less than completely, you are missing out on "true" blessing. God promises that if we trust in him, that if we have faith in him, we will have want of nothing. Remember the passage of Luke 6:36-38 that was cited in Step #2–Tithing?

> Be compassionate as your Father is compassionate. Do not judge and you will not be judged yourselves; do not condemn, and you will not be condemned yourselves; grant pardon and you will be pardoned. Give and there will be gifts for you: A full measure pressed down, shaken together and running over, will be poured into your lap; because the amount you measure out is the amount you will be given back.

The mental picture of that last scripture is powerful, "A full measure pressed down, shaken together and running over will be poured into your lap!"

Can you imagine what that type of blessing would look like? A "full measure," not skimpy, not half, not even "almost full," but "full"! Not fluffy full, not short in any manner whatsoever, pressed down so that there is no doubt that it is a "full" measure, heaping and running over. Does this not give you a better picture of what God is promising to his children?

Have you experienced or felt that your prayers were not being heard? There are only a few reasons why this occurs. First, you ask wrongly. God asks that you approach him humbly and sincerely. You must take the time to develop your relationship through prayer and you must remember to add, "Please, let your will be done, not mine!"

Second, it will cause some sort of hurt or harm. Since God is all knowing and all seeing he will never give something that will harm or hurt his children. You should seek to have God reveal the impact of what you ask for.

Third, you do not ask enough or sometimes at all! Too many times people forget to ask for what they need or they ask for it one time or perhaps for only a short while. If you *really* need something, you must ceaselessly ask for it, even if that means for a year or longer. Then you must be ready to receive whatever the answer may be—positive or negative!

Fourth, you may not be right with God. You may have sin or wrongdoing that is keeping your prayers from being heard. Atone for any sin or wrongdoing you may have committed, and perform penance or an act of contrition.

What Your Children Should Know about Giving and Saving Abundantly

Teaching your children how to be "exceptional" givers and savers is a necessary step to becoming a "true" steward. You must teach your children to become savers before they can become "exceptional" givers because your children cannot give what they do not have. They can't expect to be "blessed" if they do not give. They cannot save what they have already spent. They cannot expect "increase" if they do not save. You must teach your children that if they practice diligence in both giving and saving, they will be both blessed and wealthy.

Giving and Saving in Abundance–In Review

Mastering giving and perfecting savings are the focus of this 8th and final step. Making the practice of the Law of Reciprocity (sowing and reaping) your focus, is key to becoming a faithful steward. God expects us to be givers. To become an effective giver you must make life changing commitments such as:

1. Honoring God with your life, to aid in character development

2. Discover why God has chosen to bless you with more financial resources than is needed. God does this to test your character.

3. Honor God with your wealth. There is nothing more revealing about a person's character than the uses to which you employ your money [21]

To become an effective saver and investor you must learn to trust God. You must believe in your God-given talents and potential. You must not cripple your success by placing limits on your ability to achieve greatness based on your self-imposed limitations. God's ways are not man's ways.

Scriptures to live by:

Leviticus 26:3–6 (If you keep God's commandments you will be blessed)

Galatians 6:7–10 (Whatever you sow you shall reap)

2 Corinthians 9:6–9 (Give what you have decided to give–God loves a cheerful giver)

Luke 8:1–4 (Giving from what is left over versus all that you have)

Mathew 19:16–22 (What must be done to inherit the kingdom of God–give)

Luke 16:9–13 (You can not be the slave of two masters)

WHAT NEXT?

You have come to the end of the eight steps. What are you thinking? Do you see your future differently? Do you have hope and see light at the end of the tunnel as you should? Perhaps you feel a little overwhelmed. That's okay. Actually, it is quite normal. You should view your finances as a journey, a journey that is lifelong, a journey that should be treated with the utmost solemnity. This does not mean your journey toward becoming a "true" steward will not be full of fun, challenges, and a life of tremendous self-fulfillment; it will be!

Remember, at the beginning of the book, I stated, "To become a 'true' steward you must *master* the three stewardship principles, the principles of giving, managing, and increase." By faithfully practicing the eight steps you will be well on your way to becoming a "true" steward. Continue to focus on the eight steps. Also, focus on your attitude. Remember, suc-

cesses in personal finance are 20 percent knowledge and 80 percent attitude. Stress is an attitude!

Are you going to allow yourself to stress out on money when your finances are tight, bad, or perhaps downright ugly? What good does it do to worry yourself into having headaches, into feeling physically sick, or into an emotional frenzy, causing sleepless nights? Will doing any of this help move you one inch toward solving your financial problems? It won't! You should never engage in this behavior!

Far too many people needlessly stress out when they run into financial difficulties. This is not to say that the problems are not real problems, causing real discomfort, but *you* will choose how you feel and react to the challenges. Will you focus on actively solving all of your financial problems with a God-given solution, such as the eight steps, or will you continue along your current path, perhaps living a quiet life of financial desperation?

God, being the loving God that he is, allows us the freedom to choose a path. Your choice, however, will have consequences. Will you choose a life of blessing and prosperity and self-fulfillment, or a life of stress, worry, anxiety, and perhaps even severe financial deprivation? He wants you to choose his way.

During the period of my life that I was experiencing financial problems, but before the time we became homeless, I kept a journal of my actions, thoughts, challenges, and victories. Reading some of the most difficult and painful entries, and reflecting back on some of my darkest moments, I can honestly say I struggled with believing God could guide me through everything. I struggled with understanding how God could love a person such as myself, a person with all of my faults and failures. I struggled knowing, I struggled in believing, and I struggled with faith that God could or would guide my life financially. I now fully understand how needless and fruitless all of that worry, stress, and uncertainty were. I thought I needed to carry the load myself. I felt I had no one to turn to for strength. I felt that I could deal with the baggage on my own. I was so very wrong!

As I mentioned at the beginning of the book, your journey starts with turning over all of your fear, turning over all of your problems, turning over all of your pain and turning over *all* of your personal baggage pertaining to your financial problems to God. Your baggage might consist of financial shortcomings, such as bad habits, or an improper attitude and poor decisions or perhaps your baggage consists of a complete and total financial failure—not unlike mine. To whatever the degree of which your baggage consists, you must *never* forget, there is no limit to the mercy and grace God is capable of bestowing upon you.

You should no longer stress or worry about *how* you are going to face your financial challenges. You should no longer fear *how* things will work out. You should have confidence that God understands your distress. He understands what you need before you ask it of him. You should understand that our heav-

enly Father loves us more than we could ever know. Have comfort in knowing … in believing … in faith that God will guide you financially. It took me many years, lots of worry and lots of stress to learn this profound, yet simple truth. You have the opportunity, if you don't already know this truth, to learn this truth now (it's about who has the control).

Decide to allow God to assume control of your finances. With God in your driver's seat you have nothing to fear. With God in your driver's seat you have nothing to doubt. With God in your driver's seat you have everything to gain! All you have to do is hand over the keys.

EPILOGUE

I would strongly encourage anyone who wishes to measurably improve his/her life to read self-improvement-type books. That is the one solid constant I had in my life during my biggest tribulations. Soon after being hospitalized in February of 1993, I began to read many self-improvement books, at least one book per month. To this very day, I read *every* day, a *minimum* of one book a month. More often than not, I read two or three books per month. I have read many of these books multiple times. I can see the difference these books have made in my progression of success and attainment of my and my family's goals. As a reference, I have listed a number of my favorites and most life impacting selections. They are not listed in any particular order of importance. I hope, should you choose to read any one or perhaps all, that you will enjoy and find as much value in them as I did!

The Magic of Thinking Big—David J Schwartz, Ph.D. It takes no more energy, or ability, to think BIG than it does to think small. So why think small at all? This book helped me to begin dreaming and dreaming big again.

What Do You Say When You Talk to Yourself—Shad Helmstetter, Ph.D. Everyone will have challenges in their life at some point. The difference between someone who overcomes his challenges and someone who fails to overcome them is quite small, but that small difference makes a very big difference. If you want to increase your chances at overcoming your challenges, then you must learn how to win the war that occurs between your ears. This book will do that!

Think and Grow Rich—Napoleon Hill. It is rare to encounter a 'great' person, it is rarer still to encounter several, and have them share with you the secrets that made them great. If you wish to accomplish anything of consequence in your life, you should then seek out the people who are what you want to become, or have done what you wish to do.

How to Win Friends and Influence People—Dale Carnegie. There is no such thing as a 'self-made' millionaire or a 'self-made' success. Behind every successful person are other people. If you wish to succeed at anything, then you must learn how to reach out to others and help them acquire what they want, so that you too can achieve your goals. Read this classic and learn the principles.

The Choice—Og Mandino. This was the first self-improvement book that I owned. I had been out of the hospital for 3 days when I purchased it. Little did I know the profound impact that it would have on me! You become the product of the choices you make in life. Will you choose to pursue the truly important things in life, or will you choose to pursue the things that are not? You always have choices. Will you choose to read it?

The Greatest Salesman in the World—Og Mandino. An enjoyable story that teaches timeless success principles that might potentially change your life forever. Oh … and it has very little to do with selling!

Lincoln on Leadership—Donald T. Philips. If you seek to become a leader of any type (your family, at work, your community or beyond), then you *must* acquire the skills needed to lead. This book sheds light on the abilities and leadership principles of one of the greatest leaders in our country's history.

Legend of the Golden Scrolls—Glenn Bland. Perhaps one of the most enjoyable books on wealth principles I have read. If you wish to understand the elusive nature of wealth, you will surely enjoy this delightful tale that reveals the timeless secrets to building wealth.

Silver Boxes the Gift of Encouragement—Florence Littauer. Everyone needs encouragement, especially people who are struggling. If you wish to receive encouragement you must freely give it. The Bible speaks of providing this encouragement by saying

nothing unless it blesses the listener (Ephesians 4:29). Encourage others. I *encourage* you to read this book!

The On-Purpose Person—Kevin W. McCarthy. Do you clearly understand your purpose? If not then you *must* read this book. Understanding your purpose will provide your life with profound meaning. Living out your purpose will provide profound meaning to others' lives.

The Christmas Box—Richard Paul Evans. Great presents come in small packages. Anyone who is having difficulty in his life should seek to grow in faith and hope; remembering that there is a God that both loves and cares for you deeply; a God that cares enough to have sent the ultimate Christmas gift, the gift of life.

Foolproof Finances—David Mallonee. This is a solid book dealing with personal finances but from a biblical perspective. I enjoyed it because it reinforced many of the principles I discovered in the Bible.

After Every Wedding Comes a Marriage—Florence Littauer. A successful marriage, under the best of circumstances, is difficult. Throw in a new step-family, severe financial distress, climaxing with homelessness, and you have the makings of a marital firestorm. After failing my family financially, I needed to repair the damage done to my marriage. This book provided great insight to aid in the physical, emotional and spiritual healing my marriage required after such an ordeal.

And finally … the best self-improvement book of all!

The Bible—God

BIBLIOGRAPHY

Mallonee, David. *Foolproof Finances Financial Survival from the Bible*. Mansfield, PA: Publisher ???, 1995.

Bland, Glenn. *Legend of the Golden Scrolls Ageless Secrets for Building Wealth*. Rocklin, CA: Prima Publishing, 1994.

Pentz, Croft M. *The Complete Book of Zingers*. Carol Stream, IL: Tyndale House Publishers, 1990

The Jerusalem Bible Reader's Edition. Garden City, NY: Doubleday & Company, 1968.

Index of Scriptures

Matthew 5:17
Isaiah 53:4
Isaiah 42:6–7
2 Corinthians 9:6–9
Malachi 3:8–11
Luke 6:46–49
1 Timothy 6:17–19
Deuteronomy 14:22–23
Mark 4:24–25
Haggai 1:7–10
2 Corinthians 9:6–12
Luke 6:36–38
Ecclesiasticus (Sirach) 29:15

Step #3—Pay Yourself First/Establish an Emergency Fund
Proverbs 6:6–11
Proverbs 10:5
James 4–17
Proverbs 24:3–4

Step #4—Eliminate Debt Until Only Mortgage Remains
Romans 13:8–9
Proverbs 13:11
Proverbs 10:24
Proverbs 11:2
Proverbs 30:7–9
Proverbs 11:29
Ecclesiasticus (Sirach) 18:30–33
Ecclesiasticus (Sirach) 20:12
Proverbs 15:27
Proverbs 28:13

Habakkuk 2:7
Ecclesiasticus (Sirach) 19:1
Matthew 6:25–34 (referenced only)
Proverbs 28:13
Proverbs 16:8

Step #5—A Fully Funded Emergency Fund (Six Months of Income)
Ecclesiastes 3:1–8 (referenced only)
Proverbs 22:7
Proverbs 24:30–34
Luke 13:22 (referenced only)

Step #6—Fully Implement Retirement Savings
Genesis 26:12–14
Matthew 13:4–9
Ecclesiasticus (Sirach) 29:11
Proverbs 17:16
Proverbs 10:17
Proverbs 13:18
Proverbs 23:12
Ecclesiastes 5:12–16
Proverbs 16:20
Proverbs 28:20
Proverbs 23:4–5
Proverbs 23:17
Proverbs 19:3
Proverbs 13:22
Ecclesiasticus (Sirach) 4:17–22

Step #7—Pay Off Mortgage
Ecclesiasticus (Sirach) 21:8–9
Proverbs 20:21

Proverbs 24:27
Proverbs 15:19
1 Kings 3:4–15
Proverbs 1:1–7
Proverbs 13:20
Proverbs 19:20
Proverbs 11:1 (referenced only)

Step #8—Give and Save in Abundance
Leviticus 26:3–6
Leviticus 26:9–10
Genesis 9:1
Galatians 6:7–10
Matthew 6:25–34
2 Corinthians 9:10–12
Luke 8:1–4
Acts 20:35
Ecclesiasticus (Sirach) 4:1–11
Ecclesiasticus (Sirach) 12:1, 2
Matthew 6:19–21 (referenced only)
Luke 6:43–45
Proverbs 21:13
Matthew 19:16–22
Mark 6:24
Luke 5:11
Matthew 25:14–30
Matthew 19:23–26
Luke 16:9–13
Luke 6:36–38

Epilogue
Ephesians 4:29 (referenced only)

ENDNOTES

1   Pentz p.237

2   Pentz p. ???

3   Pentz p. 213

4   Cardweb.com and MyVesta.org

5   Pentz p. 210

6   CreditCards.com–History of credit cards

7   Pentz p. 204

8   Pentz p. ???

9   Pentz p. 78

10   Pentz p. 212

11   Pentz p. 212

12   Pentz p. 207

13   Pentz p.211

14   Pentz p. 212

15   Pentz p. 209

16   Pentz p. 257

17   Pentz p. 204

18   Pentz p. 209

19   Pentz p. 208

20   Bland p.92

21   Bland p. 92

Contact Information

Mr. Zordani would love to receive any questions or comments you may have regarding his work *Faith Finances-A Guide To Mastering The Three Biblical Principles Of Financial Success In Eight Steps.* He may be contacted at:

Faith Finances
C/O Thomas Zordani
4860 Chambers Rd. #113
Denver, CO 80239

www.faithfinances.net

http://blog.faithfinances.info

For information on speaking/teaching engagements for your parish, church, organization or group provided by Mr. Zordani; you may contact *Faith Finances* by calling (720) 273-5851.

listen|imagine|view|experience

AUDIO BOOK DOWNLOAD INCLUDED WITH THIS BOOK!

In your hands you hold a complete digital entertainment package. Besides purchasing the paper version of this book, this book includes a free download of the audio version of this book. Simply use the code listed below when visiting our website. Once downloaded to your computer, you can listen to the book through your computer's speakers, burn it to an audio CD or save the file to your portable music device (such as Apple's popular iPod) and listen on the go!

How to get your free audio book digital download:

1. Visit www.tatepublishing.com and click on the e|LIVE logo on the home page.
2. Enter the following coupon code:
   11a6-681a-e102-2689-a044-a80b-6974-5e96
3. Download the audio book from your e|LIVE digital locker and begin enjoying your new digital entertainment package today!